David Osmond was born in Newport and educated at Newport High School. He obtained an MA in Local History at Cardiff University in 1994, and has had a long-term interest in the Chartist movement. This is his first book.

THE CHARTIST RAMBLER

William Edwards of Newport 1796-1849

David Osmond

Six Points Cardiff
14 Coryton Rise,
Cardiff,
South Wales,
CF14 7EJ

www.sixpointscardiff.com

First published in 2021

Reissued in 2023

Cover design by Andy Dark
Layout by Tomos Osmond

Printed and bound by Y Lolfa,
Talybont, Ceredigion, SY24 5HE

ISBN 978-1-9196448-0-6

William Edward's Newport 1838 - 1849

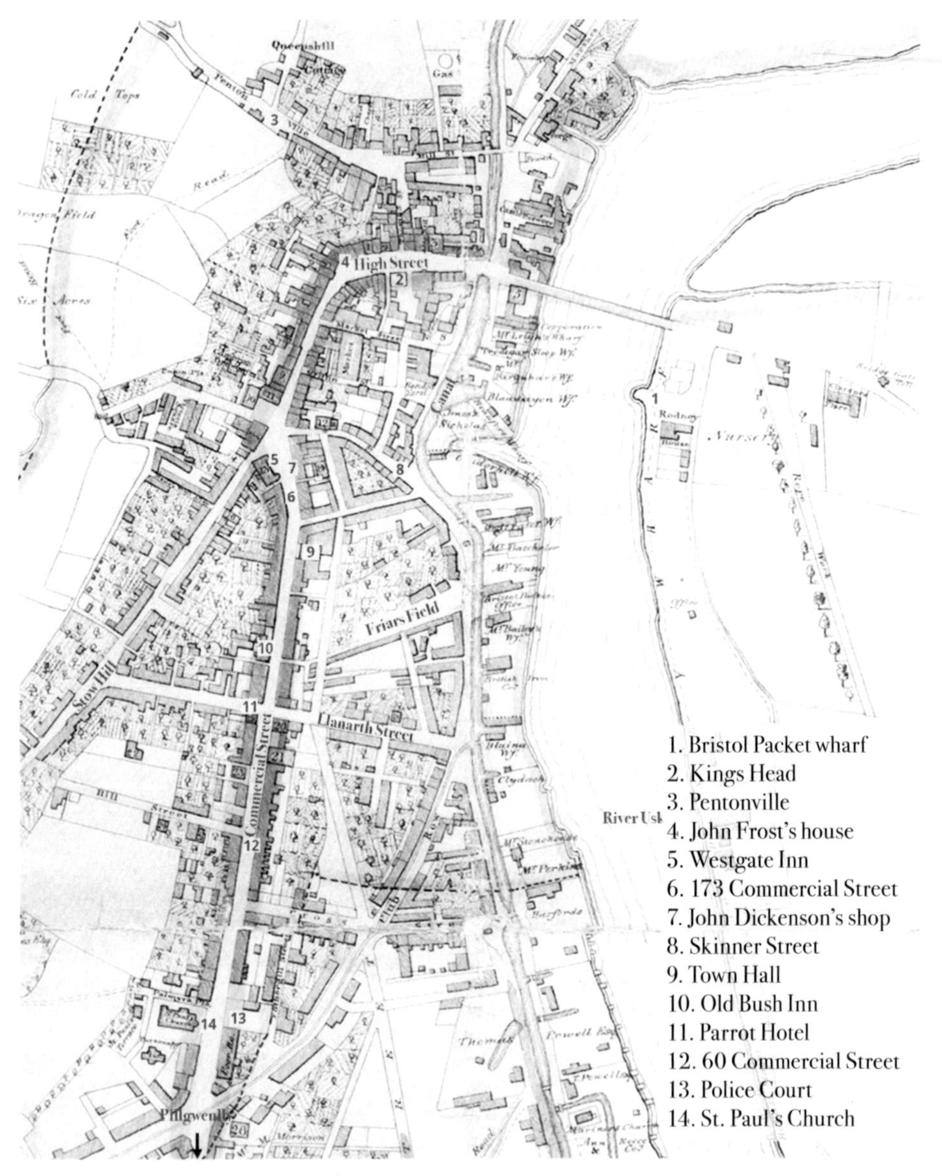

Based on 'Plan of Newport from actual survey 1836' by John Wood

CONTENTS

Haste happy day that time I long to see
When every son of Adam shall be free[1]

Isaac Watts (1674 - 1748)

INTRODUCTION

For a brief period in November 1839 the unpretentious town of Newport in South Wales was the 'Cockpit of the Kingdom'.[2] The Newport Rising, the last attempt at armed revolution on British soil, which aimed to impose universal male suffrage and the other demands of the People's Charter by force, shook the establishment locally and in London.[3] But after the successful defence of the Westgate Inn by troops of the 45th Regiment the Rising failed, and the Government acted quickly to restore order. An enhanced military presence in South Wales in the following weeks and months helped to prevent any further outbreaks.

Although a considerable amount has been written about the Newport Rising by historians and others, there is much more to the story of 19th century South Wales radicalism in general and Chartism in particular than the admittedly dramatic events of November 4th 1839: indeed too much focus on the Rising has distracted from the efforts of the many people in the area who worked throughout their lives to further the cause of democracy and political reform. William Edwards, the subject of this study, was one of those people: he was in gaol during the planning, execution and aftermath of the march on Newport but he made a crucial contribution to the growth of Chartism in South Wales, and was active in continuing the struggle after the debacle of November 1839 until his death a decade later. If he is remembered at all today it is the crazy demagogue portrayed in the pages of the local press during the peak period of his campaigning in 1839 who comes to mind, but by the end of this book it should be clear to the reader that he was a much more serious and significant figure than that.

An examination of his story gives an insight into life in general in Newport in the 1840s during a period of rapid expansion and change, and also into the wider

Bristol Steam Packet Wharf, Newport, in the 1840s

history of the districts along both the Welsh and English sides of the Severn estuary. Although Edwards is seen as a man of Newport he was born near Chepstow, married in Bristol, and lived near Stroud in the 1820s before moving to the boom town on the River Usk, probably in the mid 1830s. His life and career illustrate the strong connections across the area at that time. Bristol, with a population of around 60,000 in 1801 rising to more than 110,000 in 1841,[4] was the *de facto* capital of South Wales, while Stroud had a significant woollen industry and a strong radical tradition. There were good transport links in the region: in particular several boats ran daily ferry services between Newport and Bristol from the 1820s.[5] John Frost was selected as a parliamentary candidate in 1839 by the Stroud Chartists, although the Newport Rising prevented him from ever standing, and among those killed at the Westgate was young George Shell, originally from Bristol. The Chartist *Western Vindicator* newspaper, published in Bristol, targeted readers on both sides of the Severn: its front page masthead claimed it to be 'A bold, uncompromising advocate of the people of Bristol, Bath, Trowbridge, Bradford, Frome, Wootton-under-Edge, Newport, Pontypool, Caerleon, Cardiff, and other towns and villages in the West of England and South Wales'.[6] The rise of the iron and coal industries in South Wales in the early decades of the 19th century attracted people from a wide area, including many from the West of England, and the decline in the fortunes of Stroud and its environs in the 1820s would have contributed to this, possibly pushing Edwards into his move back to his native county. We know far more about his life and activities after his arrival in Newport, but it is important to remember that the majority of his years were spent elsewhere.

Two Scenes from a Public Life

During the febrile Chartist Spring of 1839 a tall and imposing figure became familiar in the streets of Newport and the adjoining rapidly-growing riverside township of Pillgwenlly. William Edwards, a baker with a sideline selling radical newspapers and scurrilous magazines, dubbed the 'mad baker' by the vehemently anti-Chartist *Monmouthshire Merlin*, was a vigorous and forceful advocate for the principles of the People's Charter, a tireless orator capable of speeches of more than two hours in length. When Henry Vincent, the glamorous, charismatic Chartist missionary embarked on a gruelling tour of Monmouthshire and the West of England in February, Edwards accompanied him on the Welsh section, often sharing a platform. A number of meetings took place in Newport, and Serjeant Talfourd, the prosecuting barrister at Edwards's trial at Monmouth Assizes in August 1839 for conspiracy and unlawful assembly, painted a vivid pied-piper picture of the big man striding through the evening streets, sometimes brandishing a stick, gathering supporters and leading them to the open space in Pentonville and Mill Street where public gatherings were held. Vincent addressed the crowd there from the back of a waggon positioned under a gas lamp, and Edwards would sometimes call encouragement from the midst of the throng.[7] Vincent was immensely popular, and in his 'Life and Rambles', a diary of his travels published in the *Western Vindicator*, he described how on one occasion when he left on the steam packet[8] to Bristol from the wharf just below Newport Bridge, shipwrights and seamen along the river bank stopped work and cheered as he passed downriver.[9]

Two years later an angry raucous mob gathered in those same streets on the night following the Monmouth Boroughs poll in the 1841 General Election. Their passions inflamed by the words of a fellow radical and former friend of Edwards, led by a drummer and bearing an effigy of the veteran radical, later hanged and set on fire, they paraded through the town and attacked his house and business premises in Commercial Street causing considerable damage. The carnage only ended deep into the night with the intervention of the military, after the local police decided that discretion was the better part of valour.

These two scenes illustrate some of the fluctuating fortunes of a colourful public life lived through a turbulent period in the history of Newport and its Monmouthshire hinterland. But Edwards's story began in the quiet of the 18th century Gwent countryside, a world away from the boisterous streets of the flourishing industrial port where it ended.

When I was very young my attachment to liberty subjected me to much persecution...[10]

William Edwards

EARLY LIFE

The basic details of Edwards's early life can be gleaned from baptism and marriage records and from the very brief account he gave of his younger days in 'The Life and Rambles of W. Edwards of Newport, Chartist Agitator, written by himself', two articles which were published in the *Western Vindicator* in April 1839.[11] He was born at Llanguilan Farm in the tiny agricultural village of Itton,[12] three and a half miles north-west of Chepstow, in 1796 and was baptised in St Deiniol's Church in Itton on November 20th in the same year.[13] His parents, John and Mary, were in their thirties at the time of his birth, and William was the sixth of their seven children.[14] The second oldest, Mary, born in 1789, also became involved in the Chartist movement in Newport: she is commemorated in a mosaic mural in St Paul's Walk, off Commercial Street, which was unveiled in 2018. It is interesting in the light of the debate about whether Monmouthshire was in Wales or England, that despite coming from an Anglicised corner of the county, Edwards considered himself to be Welsh.[15] There is no record of his education, but he became literate enough to write pamphlets, letters to newspapers, and articles for the *Western Vindicator* containing numerous scriptural references, quotations from Thomas Paine and other notable radicals, and Latin aphorisms, so it is possible that he attended one of the schools which existed in Chepstow at the time of his childhood.[16] Edwards's two elder brothers both died at the age of eighteen, Thomas in 1808 and John in 1813: his younger brother Charles only lived a little longer and after his demise in 1824 at the age of twenty five, William was the sole surviving son.[17]

In his 'Rambles' he professed an 'attachment to liberty' from a very young age, which resulted in 'much persecution by those who are near and dear relatives', but his real political awakening occurred at the age of 19 at the end of the Napoleonic Wars, when he became aware of 'the awful condition of the working classes of this country' during the post-war agricultural and economic depression, and resolved 'to ramble from place to place to rouse them, to seek for and demand their rights'. Disillusion followed: he was 'deceived many times', in particular by the Whigs, who 'promised us good laws but have given us bad ones'. 'Disgusted by the conduct of the House of Commons', he resolved to abandon any involvement with politics, despairing 'of ever having a good home... good laws, of the masses of the people ever being represented'.[18]

On January 26th 1821 at the age of 23 he married Sarah Stiff, who was four years younger than him, at St James's Church in Bristol. The curate, Charles Back, officiated and the witnesses were Thomas and Elizabeth Davey, who performed this function at many marriages at the church.[19] By 1826 the Edwards's were living in the village of Whiteshill near Stroud, and on November 12th Sarah gave birth there to a daughter, Mary Ann. She was baptised on December 31st at Stroud Old Meeting House, an Independent chapel.[20] The Independents, one of the three categories of Dissent recognised and licensed by the Toleration Act of 1688-89 together with the Presbyterians and the Baptists, were made up of autonomous congregations which were not subject to governance by any outside authority. They operated a democratic system in which the members of each church decided on the form of worship to be used and elected their officers, including the minister.[21] Many Independents became Chartists, and the nature of his faith undoubtedly influenced Edwards's political beliefs. Nothing is known of the religious affiliation of his parents, but it is interesting to speculate whether he was brought up as a member of the denomination or came to it by choice as an adult.

William and Sarah had at least one other child. The will of John Edwards, William's father, made in March 1831, included William's son John as a beneficiary.[22] Sarah mentioned two children in a petitioning letter written on her husband's behalf in 1841 when he was in Oakham Gaol. Mary Ann, then aged 14, was the only child to appear in the entry for the family in the 1841 census and it is likely that John was older and had left home by then.

Although in 1841 Edwards wrote that he had been a shopkeeper for twenty years, the record of Mary Ann's baptism in 1826 listed her father's occupation as 'Preacher of the Gospel'. It would obviously have been possible to combine both roles and his preaching would probably have been a part-time pursuit: maybe he used it for the purposes of the baptism register to emphasise his religious credentials.[23] At some point in the next twelve years the family joined the migration from the countryside to the towns and cities that was taking place in the first few decades of the 19th century - the percentage of the population of England and Wales living in rural areas declined from 65.4 in 1801 to 54.1 in 1841 - and by 1838 they were living in Newport where Edwards was working as a grocer and baker, supplementing his income by the sale of radical books, newspapers and periodicals.[24] Possibly they followed Edwards's sister Mary Brewer to the town. The death of his father John in 1833 may also have had an influence, although the only direct financial legacy left to Edwards in his father's will was a sum of £50 for apprenticing and educating his children, with a further payment of £50 to William himself to be made twelve months after his mother's death: she survived for another six years so this second payment would not have been made until May 1840.[25] In 1835 there were twelve bakers in Newport according to *Pigot's Directory of Monmouthshire*, none of them named William Edwards, so it is likely that the move occurred between 1835 and 1838. Edwards's career as a baker ended with his gaol sentence and he did not resume it when he returned to Newport in 1841 after his release, though he operated a bookselling and stationery business in Commercial Street for the rest of his life.

The family arrived in a town which was increasing dramatically in size and population as a result of the rapid development of the South Wales iron and coal industries. The opening of the Monmouthshire Canal in 1796 was the key to its growth, and the town lay on the west bank of the tidal River Usk, which was capable of accommodating a large volume of shipping at riverside wharves south of the Town Bridge, and in the Town Dock once it was completed in 1842 after seven years of construction work. Coal shipments from Newport rose from 29,981 tons in 1801 to 603,159 in 1851, and the tonnage of iron carried on the Monmouthshire Canal increased from 1,091 in 1802 to 219,199 in 1846.[26] The population grew from just over one thousand in 1801 to 10,492 at the time of the 1841 census, but the true figure was considerably higher as Newport had spread beyond its old boundaries into the parishes of St Woolos and Christchurch. Even so, the official figures made Newport the third largest urban settlement in Wales after Merthyr Tydfil and

Swansea.[27] From the nucleus of the medieval town between the castle and St Woolos Church, Newport expanded to the south: Commercial Street and Commercial Road linked the old centre with Pillgwenlly which had grown up adjacent to the quays of the Tredegar Wharf Company and the terminus of the canal. Some substantial and elegant terraces such as Victoria Place (1842) and Clifton Place were built on high ground on Stow Hill, but much of the population lived on the low lying land along the river, often in overcrowded courts and lodging houses in areas like Friars Field and Pillgwenlly, where sanitation and drainage were major problems. The Clarke Report into the sanitary conditions of the town, published in 1850, painted a vivid street-by-street picture of the squalor in which many of the townspeople lived. The report demonstrated the link between poverty, overcrowding, poor drainage and disease, and in 1841 the mortality rate in Pillgwenlly was worse than that in Liverpool.[28] Despite the difficult conditions endured by many of its people, throughout the 1830s and 1840s Newport began to acquire the institutions and infrastructure appropriate for the significant town that it had become. A considerable number of public, commercial and religious buildings were completed including Mynydd Sion Chapel (1835), St Pauls Church (1836), St Marys Church (1840), the Town Hall (1842), the Baptist Temple, Commercial Road (1843), the cattle market (1844), Raglan Barracks (1845), and the South Wales Railway, running from Chepstow to Swansea (1846). Banks and benefit societies were established; a dispensary opened in 1839; British, National and several private schools provided for the educational needs of at least part of the population, and cultural institutions for adults such as Newport Mechanics Institute (1840) and Newport Choral Society (1846) were founded. Local government too had changed significantly in 1835, when the Municipal Corporations Act was adopted, extending the franchise considerably for local elections.[29]

Chartism was often at its strongest in small manufacturing towns dominated by one industry, particularly where the workers were threatened by modernisation, rather than in larger urban centres with a more mixed industrial base.[30] Newport, though large in Welsh terms, was a small town by English standards, but its development as a port and centre of commerce had given it a wide variety of industries and trades. Although its working classes lacked the overwhelming commonality of interest possessed by those in other places such as the textile towns of the North of England,

Chartism exerted a powerful and sustained influence in Newport for a decade from the late 1830s. Despite his earlier disenchantment with political activism, the growth of the campaign for the People's Charter in 1838 rekindled Edwards's enthusiasm and he threw himself into the new movement with all the vigour he could muster.

I will go upon the Welsh hills...
and illuminate all the country around[31]

William Edwards

CHARTIST ADVOCATE
1838 - MAY 1839

Newport Working Men's Association

After the disappointment of the modest extension of the franchise from 10% to 18% of the adult male population which resulted from the so-called Great Reform Act of 1832, radicals continued to campaign for more substantial changes to Britain's electoral system.[32] In June 1836 the first meeting of the London Working Men's Association (LWMA) took place in Covent Garden: among those present were William Lovett and Francis Place, the old radical tailor of Charing Cross. Rules and aims were agreed, and these included the pursuit of equal political and social rights for all classes. Lovett was the principal architect of the document which later became known as the People's Charter, which was published in the form of a draft parliamentary bill in May 1838 with a preamble by J. A. Roebuck, at that time the Radical MP for Bath. The bill set out six changes which the authors believed would lead to a fairer electoral system and a parliament much more representative of the people, the famous Six Points.[33] It was publicly launched on May 21st at a meeting in Glasgow attended by 200,000 people including LWMA delegates, and a proposal of the Birmingham Political Union that signatures should be collected for a National Petition in support of the Six Points was adopted. Later in 1838 the decision was made to convene a National Convention of the Industrious Classes to co-ordinate strategy and to supervise the collection of signatures and the presentation of the Petition to the House of Commons by sympathetic MPs in the summer: it met in London for the first time on February 4th 1839.[34]

The LWMA encouraged the formation of similar groups in towns and cities throughout the country, often with the help of 'missionaries' dispatched to get things

Samuel Etheridge

started. According to William Edwards, he and 'a few other working men' formed the Newport Working Men's Association in July 1838, with rules based on those of the LWMA, but there is no evidence to indicate the involvement of a London emissary in this case.[35] A copy of the Rule Book of NWMA survives and is held in Newport Reference Library: it was printed by John Partridge, in whose house John Frost was arrested after the Rising. It was the second WMA to be set up in Monmouthshire - Pontypool was the first - and the membership grew rapidly, reaching 'nearly six hundred, besides a prosperous Female Association' by April 1839.[36] In January 1839 printer Samuel Etheridge, who had been involved in local radical politics for many years, was the secretary, and grocer and draper Edward Thomas had succeeded James Horner as treasurer. Meetings were usually held in public houses including the Royal Oak in Thomas Street, the Old Bush, the Ship and Pilot and the Parrot in Commercial Street, and the Devonshire House in Dock Parade in Pillgwenlly. We know a few details about the regular weekly meetings: contributions of one penny per week were collected from members as they arrived at the association's room, and then business began with the appointment of a chairman for the evening, followed by speeches.[37] Several larger meetings were reported by the *Monmouthshire Merlin*. On October 23rd at the Old Bush Inn 'upwards of 150 members' discussed the Charter: the meeting ended with a summary of the proceedings in Welsh. A week later more than four hundred people squeezed into the Great Room behind the Parrot Hotel to listen to John Frost and Edwards explain the Six Points; and on November 30th Edwards addressed a meeting at the Devonshire House which chose Frost as the delegate to the National Convention for Newport and Caerleon. Meanwhile on November 12th Edwards was in Caerleon, where he spoke 'at length' at the inaugural meeting of the Caerleon Working Men's Association in the 'large room' at the George Inn in High Street, which culminated in the enrolment of 35 members.[38]

Newspaper Agent

Edwards played another important part in the development of Chartism in Newport through his role as an agent for the sale of Chartist newspapers. Titles such as the *Northern Star* and the *Western Vindicator* provided political news and disseminated information about the aims and tactics of the movement to a wide audience, and were a necessary counterbalance to the hostility to Chartism exhibited by most of the mainstream press. Distribution of the newspapers was dependent on a network of vendors, of whom Edwards was one: an advertisement by the publisher of the *Vindicator* in the *Bristol Times* on May 4th 1839 listed nineteen agents scattered across the West of England and South Wales including Edwards and James Horner in Newport. Copies of the newspapers reached their audiences by a variety of means: many were bought and read by individuals, but sometimes several people would club together to meet the cost, and many descriptions exist of extracts being read aloud to groups in homes or public houses, sometimes by children who had better literacy skills than their parents.[39] In Newport, readings from the *Northern Star* took place in the Prince of Wales on Cardiff Road and the Queen Adelaide in Griffin Street.[40] Edwards continued to sell newspapers throughout the 1840s.

Promoting the Charter: January - May 1839

In December 1838 the LWMA chose Henry Vincent, a 25 year old printer from London, as a roving missionary given the tasks of promoting the Charter in the West of England and South-east Wales, and collecting signatures for the National Petition.[41] He got to work quickly, and on January 1st 1839 he was a guest speaker at a meeting held in Pontnewynydd, called to discuss the Charter and to nominate John Frost as the representative for Pontypool at the National Convention - as we have seen Frost had already been chosen as the delegate for Newport and Caerleon. The meeting had been advertised on printed placards and was preceded by a parade around Pontypool led by a band; some people carried banners displaying slogans such as 'Universal Suffrage' and 'Vote by Ballot'. The crowd, some seven or eight hundred strong, gathered on the ground outside John Llewellyn's beer house, where temporary hustings leaning against the back of the building had been created. William Edwards took the chair, having been proposed by Frost, who then addressed the gathering before handing over to Vincent.[42] It seems that it was during this New Year visit to Monmouthshire that Edwards met Vincent for the first time, the start of a close association that lasted for several years.

Their next recorded meeting was on January 27th at a gathering of Working Men's Association delegates from South Wales and the West of England at the rooms of Bath WMA. Edwards addressed the group, and promised that he would 'go upon the Welsh Hills, and by the bright intelligence he had received that day, he would illuminate all the country around', a pledge which was greeted by 'tremendous cheering'. He denounced the use of physical force, and said that the biggest obstacle faced by the Newport Chartists was the reluctance of local electors to forego their election-time bribes. Later that evening Edwards seconded a resolution proposed by Vincent, before the delegates adjourned for dinner to the Chequers Inn, where 'some patriotic songs were sung'.[43]

Edwards was true to his word and a week later he embarked on a period of intensive campaigning in Newport and the industrial valleys of Monmouthshire which lasted until his arrest on May 10th. On his first few visits to the 'hills' he was accompanied by Edward Thomas, who was a Welsh speaker, making him a useful addition to the platform. Thomas was described as 'very eloquent and impressive' by the *Northern Star*, which is not surprising as he was also a noted Chartist poet, many of whose verses were published in the *Western Vindicator*.[44] Vincent made three visits of six, four and nine days to the county during this period, and he was usually accompanied by Edwards when he spoke at meetings in a variety of locations.[45] They also both addressed a gathering of Bristol Chartists on February 28th at the room of the local Working Men's Association.[46] They must have made an odd couple: Vincent slim and young and Edwards larger and much older and coarser, perhaps a little like Tony Blair and John Prescott in more recent years. In a letter to the *Northern Star*, written in November 1840 from Oakham Gaol, Edwards claimed that his exertions on behalf of the Charter in the spring of 1839 had cost him 'at least fifty pounds of my own money': he even personally took signatures for the petition collected in Monmouthshire to London in time for the planned submission to Parliament on May 6th.[47] He was obviously unable to work as a baker when travelling around the area, but his wife continued to sell newspapers and radical magazines in Newport when he was away with the help of her sister-in-law, Mary Brewer.

One April week of non-stop campaigning in Vincent's company exemplified Edwards's commitment to the cause. After arriving in Newport from Bristol on the

Henry Vincent

18th, Vincent was 'conducted amidst cheering to the house of my friend Edward Thomas'. On the evenings of the 18th and 19th Edwards rallied support for mass open-air meetings held in Pentonville in Newport, before riding to Pontypool the next morning, where he was one of the speakers who addressed a crowd of several thousand '... in an able manner... and was well received'. Chartists attended St Pauls Church in Newport *en masse* on Sunday 21st, where they listened to a sermon outlining the folly of their ways from the Rev. James Francis: Vincent was present and it seems highly likely that Edwards was in the congregation as well. The occupation of reserved pews in parish churches before services was a tactic used fairly widely by Chartists in 1839 to draw attention to their cause: in some cases they behaved irreverently, wearing hats and smoking, but in others they sought to portray their respectability by the dignity of their conduct.[48] On Monday the two men travelled by gig to Pontllanfraith and then walked to Gelligroes for the first of three meetings that day; they returned to the Coach and Horses in Blackwood for the second, chaired by Dr William Price, before riding to the Greyhound in Pontllanfraith for the final rally held outside in heavy rain. On April 23rd they rode to Nantyglo for a meeting at the King Crispin, and then walked to the Royal Oak in Blaina, where they addressed a gathering that evening on a hill behind the pub. Edwards described the two landlords, David Lewis and Zephaniah Williams as '... two of the best Chartists I ever met'.[49] Another journey on horseback the next day took them via Abergavenny to Pontypool where a crowd of thousands turned up to hear them. Their hectic week ended on Thursday April 25th when they rode back to Newport for a meeting that evening in Pentonville.[50]

Meetings were often accompanied by a considerable amount of ceremonial. Placards were posted in public places advertising the event, and the town crier would sometimes be used to drum up support. Sometimes the main meeting was preceded by a parade. On May 1st, a procession headed by a band, followed by women and children and then men, all arranged in ranks of five, with echoes of the military organisation later used by the marchers on Newport in November, walked from Blackwood to the Star Inn in Dukestown near Tredegar. Edwards and the other speakers travelled in a chaise with a Union Jack hung above them and the chaise was later used as the hustings at the meeting which took place in a field in front of the pub. Banners were carried by some of those participating.[51] On March 26th Vincent and Edwards walked from

Pontllanfraith to Blackwood where they were escorted into the town by one hundred girls carrying flowers and singing radical songs: that evening they returned to the Greyhound where they were entertained by harp music.[52]

Many of the meetings were held outside, either because no rooms large enough to accommodate the numbers attending were available or because of the reluctance of the authorities or the landlords of public houses to allow meetings to take place on their premises. In many cases Vincent and Edwards estimated the size of their audiences: for example, Vincent claimed that five to six thousand attended the Blaina meeting on April 23rd, ten to twelve thousand were in the streets of Pontypool the next day, and another eight thousand massed at Pentonville on the 25th.[53] The anti-Chartist *Monmouthshire Merlin* tended to downplay the numbers: a correspondent claimed that 'but few' attended a Pontypool meeting on April 12th for which Edwards claimed a crowd of 4,000, and the *Merlin* estimated that 800 were at Dukestown on May 1st, while Edwards claimed that a highly improbable 30,000 had been present.[54] It is reasonable to conclude that these were frequently large gatherings of hundreds and sometimes thousands of people, but it is impossible to be more precise. It is worth noting too that the weather was often unkind to the Chartists and a number of the open air rallies took place in heavy rain: on February 12th Edwards addressed a large meeting in a field in Crosspenmaen in a downpour, with the *Northern Star* reporting on the 'most singular appearance' created by the umbrellas held by most of his audience.[55]

In April and May at least six public meetings were held in Pentonville in Newport, and eyewitness descriptions survive in the evidence presented at the trial of Vincent, Edwards, and two other local Chartists, William Townsend, a 24 year old wine merchant, and John Dickenson, a butcher, at Monmouth in August. The meeting held on April 19th can serve as an example. Watkin Richards, the harbourmaster, was in Llanarth Street at about 7 o'clock in the evening when he saw a crowd of around 200 people moving along Commercial Street towards Pillgwenlly. Edwards was organising them into ranks of five or six abreast and some were carrying sticks. Some time later the crowd returned, now 500-700 strong. More of them were carrying sticks, some openly, others concealing them under their jackets, and one had a piece of wood seven feet long and two inches in diameter. Edwards, Vincent and Townsend were arm in arm, there was shouting and hissing and the singing of 'Britons never shall be slaves'. Thomas Hawkins, a High Street ironmonger, saw the procession passing his door on the way to Pentonville, cheering and hissing as they went, and solicitor Thomas Phillpotts of High Street, heard cheering at about 8 o'clock and saw the crowd moving up High Street towards the Kings Head Hotel. Mayor Thomas Phillips described the meeting place in Pentonville as an open area measuring about 100 yards by 15 yards, with one gas lamp which was utilised to illuminate the hustings. This site now lies at least partly under the main London to South Wales railway line and Newport station. A waggon positioned under the lamp served as a platform, and on this occasion the crowd was estimated to be about a thousand strong by Richards. Vincent spoke 'of bastiles,[56] Poor Law Commissioners and destruction of children'. Edwards was moving around amongst the crowd, and at one point proceedings were interrupted by Townsend, who said that someone was going to shoot Vincent, indicating the direction that the firing would come from. Edwards said 'something about his police', and no firing occurred. The meeting ended between 10 and 11 o'clock, with the crowd heading for John Frost's house in High Street where they cheered before dispersing.[57]

From the outset of his campaign, Edwards struck a moderate tone, explicitly repudiating physical force at Bath on the 27th January and a week later at Blackwood, and seconding a vote of thanks to 'ministers of the Gospel' who had attended a meeting on March 5th at the Old Bush Inn in Newport, called to protest about the threat to John Frost's position as a magistrate.[58] He had a reputation as an able and entertaining orator, perhaps honed during his time as a preacher. The *Northern Star* described how, at a meeting at Pontllanfraith on February 11th, Edwards's '... wonted facetious eloquence and happy mode of describing our national affairs did not on this occasion forsake him, as he set the meeting in roars of laughter'.[59] In his articles in the *Western Vindicator* Vincent often referred to Edwards's ability and popularity: at Bristol on February 28th he 'spoke fluently and with much effect'; at Pontllanfraith on March 26th 'he delivered an able speech and was loudly cheered'; and at Pontypool on April 24th he 'made a capital speech and was much cheered. He seems to be much respected by the people...'[60] Vincent was of the opinion that 'Edwards is very popular on the hills, and he has done much good by his unwearied activity'.[61] Sarah Edwards (no relation), landlady of the Greyhound Inn in Pontllanfraith, said that he attracted many recruits to the Chartist lodge based there.[62] Edwards certainly did not seem to lack in confidence. Vincent described an occasion on April 23rd when he and Edwards encountered Crawshay Bailey, the iron master, while walking from Nantyglo to Blaina: 'a running conversation took place between Mr Edwards and Bailey in which Edwards charged him with a few awkward things'.[63]

But as the 1839 spring unfolded, Edwards's rhetoric became more florid and violent. A significant factor in this change appears to have been the Devizes riot on April 1st, when Vincent and other Chartists were lucky to escape serious injury or worse at the hands of a mob, alleged by Vincent to be railway workers recruited by local Tories with the connivance of the authorities.[64] Edwards later claimed that when the news of the Devizes affair reached Newport, and the town was 'in a state of such excitement', he advised the people to keep the peace, although it was alleged that he was responsible for exciting them in the first place![65] On April 5th, with Vincent unfit to travel from the West Country, Edwards took his place as the principal speaker at a meeting in Pontypool: he admitted to being very low and miserable, but when he got to the room 'my spirits became invigorated and we had a most glorious meeting'.[66] The *Monmouthshire Merlin* took a different view, saying that Edwards 'treated his audience with one of the most extraordinary displays of eloquence ever heard'. They proceeded to list some excerpts. Edwards 'would not give a tinker's damn for any Chartist who would not stand and have his head cleaved asunder in support of the Charter'. 'Every Whig and Tory ought to have a tenpenny nail driven through his bloody heart...' 'If the Charter was not granted on the 6th of May he would not answer for the consequences. He had five thousand able fellows, like himself, at Blackwood that he could call together by a blast of his horn.'[67] Edwards denied using the words attributed to him by the *Merlin*, which he called 'that disgraceful Whig hack', but the newspaper produced five witnesses in support of their allegations.[68] Another account of Edwards's speech on this occasion was given by George Essex, who attended the meeting and was called as a prosecution witness in Edwards's second trial in March 1840. Essex took no notes, but wrote down what he could remember some thirty minutes after the event concluded, and his record gives a flavour of Edwards's rhetorical style, though its accuracy is obviously questionable:

'I was at the meeting at the King's Head on the 5th of April. I heard Edwards speak. I made notes the same evening. Edwards was speaking when I got there. He said - (Mr Essex read from his notes) - "Like the children of Israel of old in Egypt you, my friends are oppressed, and the Israelites at first were worked hard, and were paid but little; and then their oppressors, finding they put up with that, they put heavier tasks upon them and paid them not at all. So it is in this country with your oppressors, the aristocracy. The Whigs and Tories imposed tasks upon you, which you bore. Finding that, they put heavier tasks, which you ought to resist if you attend to the Word of God, instead of Jack Russell and the devil's agents. The population of Britain is 22,000,000. Now how many contribute to the wealth of the country? You will be surprised to hear only 8,000,000, leaving 14,000,000, to be supported by the 8,000,000, as every poor boy, twelve years old, who goes to work hard and get his ten or twelve shillings per week, has to provide for some of those lazy, oppressive, grinding down, monkey-faced aristocrats before he is allowed to put one bit in his own mouth. Is not this oppression, and not to be borne? Some of you will say, how is it done? It would not do to send a tax-gatherer to take twelve shillings out of every pound they earn, so they put on an indirect taxation, as the excise, so that they tax what you eat and what you wear, and every little enjoyment. Have I not proved that you are oppressed? I am sure you will no longer submit to this. God has seen how you have been ground down, as he did the Israelites, and has taken compassion, and has raised up for you those who shall lead you forth like the children of Israel: and I shall, I hope, give you no reason to grumble at me, as the children of Israel did with Moses, and if you do not obtain your rights, something more than their doorposts shall be marked with blood, my brethren and sisters, by the command of God. When the Israelites went forth from their oppressors they despoiled them," and, he added in a very loud voice, "the property of this country is yours, and belongs to you, and God calls on you to go forward and take it, and it has been with your oppressors long enough.

God is with you. What have you to fear? and as God is superior to the devil, and whopped him, you will be, with his assistance, able to whop his agents, your enemies, the grinding down Whigs and Tories", and he (Mr Edwards) looked round and said, "Now Mr Tory, don't quarrel with me for telling the people to go to take the property. Recollect it is the word of God." As to the soldiers, he said they would out with the aristocracy officers, and promotion from the ranks would follow, and the soldiers, instead of hurting them, would every man plunge his sword into the earth: and if promotion had been from the ranks some in the room would have been generals, and would be better than the monkey-faced aristocracy. He said the Poor Laws were concocted by Brougham, one of the Poor Law Commissioners, and the devil. And he detailed a supposed conversation between those three, which from a noise in the room I could not hear. Mr Edwards went on, "As to arming, I recommend you to follow the advice of the Morning Chronicle several years ago. They advised arming men, because it suited the purposes of the Whigs. As regards myself, I shall be prepared. I shall be active and exert my body and soul in the cause indefatigably till the 6th of May, when I shall sit down in my chair and keep my eye on the Parliament, on the Convention, and on the people, and then I shall be ready to do anything and everything to set the people free, even if it is with the sacrifice of my life." In allusion to Devizes, he said that if he had been there, and had had a bludgeon with some lead in the end of it, he would have knocked out the brains of some of them, and he added, "I have sworn to my wife - I have sworn to my children - I have sworn the limbs of my body to the mental faculties of my soul, to be free, or perish in the attempt." This speech produced considerable effect, and the people answered to several parts of it by saying "amen", as they do in some chapels.'[69]

If this report is true, Edwards at this point was advocating the seizure of property and mutiny in the army, albeit using Biblical justification. Further evidence of his change in tone comes from subsequent meetings in April and early May. At Brynmawr on April 23rd, according to the *Glamorgan, Monmouth and Brecon Gazette and Merthyr Guardian*, Edwards talked of 'cutting throats', while drawing his forefinger repeatedly across his own.[70] The *Merlin* said that his speech at Dukestown on May 1st was 'one of his raving farragos... He tore away for a couple of hours. It was horrible', while at Risca on the following day 'the exhibition he made was, we are informed, even more disgusting than that of the day before'. According to the correspondent, William Jones, later one of the leaders of the Newport Rising, who had appeared at both meetings, 'openly repudiated him... as disgraceful even to Chartism'.[71] Then, on May 18th after Edwards had been arrested, the *Merlin* published a letter from Samuel Etheridge, still the secretary of the Newport and Pillgwenlly WMA, addressed to 'the inhabitants of Newport and its vicinity'. Etheridge acknowledged the contribution that Edwards had made to the Chartist cause, but 'denounced all such violent language and conduct as he has been using towards those that are opposed to us... his zeal having outrun his knowledge on subjects of a political nature'.[72] Etheridge eventually resigned in June, and Edward Thomas also gave up his post as treasurer a month later. Thomas however continued to attend lodge meetings, and although he took no part in the Rising, he testified on Frost's behalf at his trial in January 1840, where he admitted that he was a Chartist.[73]

Edwards was aware of the disquiet that his rhetoric was causing and on April 9th he called a public meeting at the Ship and Pilot in Newport. He sent the town crier around to publicise the event, and went to Pill himself to encourage workers on the construction of the new dock to attend. He put three motions to the meeting: two of them, a vote of confidence in the National Convention and a pledge to defend Vincent against his enemies when he returned to Newport, were passed unanimously. The third, asking those present to approve his conduct 'on account of some sensations having been brought against me by enemies of the cause', was merely passed 'overwhelmingly'.[74]

After paying little attention to Edwards in the early months of 1839, in April the *Merlin* and other South Wales newspapers began to feature him much more prominently in their columns. But as Edwards's speeches became more belligerent, the attitude of the press towards him changed, and they began to ridicule him and question his character and his sanity, possibly a sign that the establishment had begun

Town Dock, Newport, 1842

to fear his ability to recruit people to the Chartist cause. In a letter published in the *Merlin* on April 20th, John Morgan gave an account of a meeting held in Abersychan on April 12th. He described how, after failing to obtain a room in a public house, Edwards was reduced to addressing the crowd from a garret window of a private home, 'thrusting himself halfway through and appearing like the figurehead of a ship in a storm'. Morgan referred to him as 'the Bedlam Deserter, as they term him in our neighbourhood'. The *Merlin's* own report of another Pontypool meeting, which took place on April 20th, claimed that the crowd was composed principally of 'persons who came to enjoy a laugh at the mad antics of the baker', who 'went on in his usual style and raved away in a manner that sets all description at defiance'. According to the report, Edwards was 'better known by the title of Sir William Courtenay', and he 'delivered just such a speech as one would expect to hear from his great prototype, who finished his career in Kent'.[75] Sir William Courtenay was the assumed name of John Thom, a Cornish wine merchant who moved to Kent. After three years in the County Lunatic Asylum he became the leader of agricultural labourers protesting against low wages and the New Poor Law, and was shot and killed in an altercation with troops of the 45th Regiment at Bossenden Wood in May 1838. The 45th went on to become the defenders of the Westgate Inn during the Newport Rising.[76] A letter to the editor of the *Glamorgan, Monmouth and Brecon Gazette and Merthyr Guardian*, signed 'Sienkin ap Howell ap Edwards ap Jones' of Nantyglo, which was never published but is held in the Treasury Solicitors' papers in the National Archives, gave an eye-witness description of the meeting held in Blaina on the evening of April 23rd. The writer, Richard Bailey, nephew of Crawshay, narrated a humorous and mocking account of the proceedings, calling Edwards a 'vagabondising, levelling, infidel, radical demagogue' who sought to 'turn the world upside down'. He also hinted at financial impropriety and a liking and need for alcohol on Edwards's part.[77] At the anti-Chartist demonstration held in Coalbrookvale on April 29th, chaired by Crawshay Bailey, one of the speakers, 'J. Brown Esq.' claimed that 'mad' Edwards had recently tried to pay only ten shillings in the pound of money that he owed for flour, and that he was on the verge of bankruptcy.[78] Allegations of insanity appeared again in the *Merlin's* account of the May Day meeting at Dukestown: after lampooning Edwards's contribution to the proceedings, the report went on to state that at the end of the event 'Edwards sent round the hat... the proceeds of which he duly pocketed. He did not appear at all insane in that part of the business', thereby succeeding in accusing him of buffoonery, madness and dishonesty all within a few paragraphs.[79] The press caricature of 'Mad Edwards the Baker' has had a long afterlife: in 1989 Islwyn Borough Councillor and future Mayor Leon Gardner played the part of Mad Edwards in The Forbidden Hymn, a 'people's opera' staged at Blackwood Miners Institute to celebrate the 150th anniversary of the Newport Rising. Gardner's costume consisted of white baker's overalls and a tall chef's hat.[80]

In early May 1839 the Newport magistrates issued warrants for the arrest of Edwards, Vincent, Dickenson and Townsend, on charges related to the meetings in Pentonville in March and April. Vincent was taken into custody in London on May 7th and was brought back to Newport by mail coach. News of his arrest reached the town in advance of his arrival, causing excitement and alarm in equal measure. Coal shipments from the Monmouthshire mines were halted, and rumours were rife that the colliers were ready to march on Newport to rescue their hero. Edwards returned home on May 10th by the Bristol steam packet from his visit to London to deliver signatures for the National Petition, and found the town in 'a state of alarming excitement, not a single person being at work on either of the coal or iron stages, the shops being shut, and the people collected here and there in knots of from twenty to fifty'.[81] His arrival was greeted by a loudly cheering crowd who escorted him into High Street, where several hundred special constables were guarding the Kings Head Hotel: a fully armed detachment of the 29th Regiment of Foot was stationed further down the street in the Westgate Inn. He was arrested by Superintendent Hopkins of the Newport police force and some of his constables - according to Edwards he was 'stopped in the streets of Newport by an armed force of Whigs and Tories, beaten with bludgeons and dragged away without a warrant'[82] - and despite attempts by the crowd to release him, he was eventually taken to a room upstairs at the Kings Head where the local magistrates were assembled. Dickenson and Townsend were also there, having been arrested earlier that day: according to Frost, Dickenson was at work when he was 'seized', and his request to change his clothes had been refused.[83] Later in the afternoon Vincent arrived, and shortly afterwards the tumult from the street outside the hotel was so great that Mayor Phillips, accompanied by a body

Kings Head Hotel, Newport, 1837

of special constables, went downstairs and read the Riot Act to the crowd from the back of a donkey cart laden with flour.[84] According to Vincent, the magistrates were terrified by the increasing noise from the street: '... whenever a loud cheer arose... they trembled from head to foot, like children at the shadow of a coffee pot on a wall'.[85] John Frost, just returned from the National Convention in London, addressed the crowd from the window of his house in High Street and tried to calm the situation by urging them to return home peacefully, although the *Times* reporter considered his speech to be 'incendiary'.[86] All four prisoners were charged with 'conspiring together to produce discomfort and disaffection among Her Majesty's subjects, and unlawfully and tumultuously assembling in breach of the public peace'. According to a memoir by Henry John Davis, published in 1891, he witnessed the day's events as a young man recently arrived in Newport. He described how the magistrates, worried about the danger of the prisoners being rescued by the crowd, gave the impression that they were to be taken from the Kings Head along Thomas Street to the Clock House in Mill Street where they were to be confined. Two cordons of special constables formed a passageway across High Street to keep the crowd back. Meanwhile the prisoners had been installed in a carriage in the hotel yard, the gates of the yard were suddenly opened and the carriage sped off to Monmouth Gaol, where the four Chartists were held until their trial at the next assizes.[87]

Although my body has been bound in prisons and cells,
yet my mind has been free and unshackled.[88]

William Edwards

TRIAL AND PRISON
MAY 1839 - MARCH 1841

Acting promptly, on May 18th the *Western Vindicator* announced the launch of a Defence Fund, inviting contributions from Wales and the West of England to pay for the legal expenses of the four men. John Frost acted as the treasurer, and collected and submitted the money raised in South Wales: the amounts received were listed every week in the *Vindicator*. A considerable sum was accumulated: South Wales raised more than £250 and the West of England at least £125, together worth around £40,000 in today's terms.[89] By far the biggest contribution in South Wales came from Merthyr, but Blackwood, Pontypool and Newport also played a big part. In Newport, money was raised by the NWMA, the Female Patriotic Association, workplace groups including shoemakers and shipbuilding apprentices, and the Royal Oak pub, run by Frost's mother, but many individual donations were also noted in the newspaper.[90]

Dickenson, at 57 by some distance the eldest of the four prisoners, was released on bail on May 20th. In a letter written by Vincent on June 1st he detailed the conditions in which the remaining three Chartists were held.[91] He described the gaol as 'a fine castlefied looking building... in a very healthy position'. They had the use during the day of a room eight yards square and thirteen feet high, with a fireplace, a stone seat along one wall, a stone floor and two wooden shelves for their linen and books, which included several works by William Cobbett. The room was shared with one other prisoner, a man accused of bigamy who was also due for trial at the next assizes. Three steps gave access to an exercise yard twenty yards by ten, surrounded by a wall. They had small separate bedrooms, containing iron bedsteads with straw mattresses and 'coarse but clean bedding', and high windows, and there was a small kitchen where they could prepare their food, which they were allowed to purchase for themselves.

They had also received gifts from Monmouthshire and the West of England including 'a fine ham and half side of bacon', tea, coffee and sugar. The day began with the ringing of a bell at 6 o'clock, after which they would wash and exercise in the yard before breakfast. They were free to do as they wished during the day, before being locked up in their bed-cells again at around eight in the evening. They were allowed to wear their own clothes, were not subjected to the indignity of a forced prison haircut, and had access to writing materials.[92]

A report on the character and habits of Edwards was produced by Charles Ford, the gaoler. He considered that Edwards had behaved 'with more restraint than he had done previous to his commitment, but his violent temper and sulky habits constantly showed themselves'. He also commented that Edwards quoted Scripture frequently in letters to his family, although Ford was unaware that 'he was given to reading prior to his arrival here'.[93]

Ford's comments resonate with the language used by Edwards in *An Address to the Working Men and Women of Newport, and of the Monmouthshire Hills*, written in Monmouth Gaol and printed as a four page pamphlet by John Partridge which sold for one penny per copy.[94] The text is full of Biblical references and in places has the cadence of the preacher that he once was. Edwards compared the persecution of the early Christians for spreading the Gospel with the treatment of those seeking to promote the Charter: 'What the Gospel is to the souls of men, the People's Charter will be to their bodies'. He quoted a well known couplet from the third verse of 'In Gabriel's hand a mighty stone', a hymn by 18th century hymn-writer Isaac Watts: 'Haste happy day (that time) I long to see / When every son of Adam shall be free', a couplet that was used in anti-slavery literature. His rhetoric was inconsistent: at one point he asked his 'friends' to 'be peaceable and persevere in the use of all legal means until you have obtained your political emancipation', but then used more confrontational imagery in another scriptural reference when he says 'Those that are not with us are against us',[95] and concluded with the thought that once the Charter had been achieved, people will look back and consider that '... it was well worth while to wade through fields of blood[96] to obtain the freedom, happiness and pleasure which we now enjoy'.

Later in June Vincent applied for bail, and was taken to London by Ford for

Monmouth Gaol prior to 1865

his request to be heard by a judge in chambers. Vincent himself was required to guarantee £500 and to provide two sureties from others for £250 each. The original bail terms set at the Kings Head in Newport also included a requirement to keep the peace for twelve months, but at Vincent's request the judge agreed to change this to a commitment to be of good behaviour until the assizes. These terms were agreed and Vincent was released.[97] During his bail period he took out a dissenter's license which enabled him to 'preach' legally at meetings, something which he did on at least one occasion - he appeared at a Chartist gathering at Brandon Hill in Bristol where he spoke on the text 'Blessed are they which are persecuted for righteousness' sake'.[98]

On July 6th, under the heading 'Court News', the *Western Vindicator* announced: 'It is rumoured in fashionable circles that Messrs Townsend and Edwards intend giving a good public breakfast to a select party of friends in a few days. An extra boiling of *skilly* (thin oatmeal gruel) will be prepared for the occasion'. Presumably this referred to the expected imminent release of the remaining two prisoners on bail: in a letter addressed 'To the Working Men of Newport, Monmouthshire', from Oakham Gaol dated November 14th 1840, and published in the *Northern Star* two weeks later, Edwards wrote that his bail from Monmouth Gaol before his first trial had cost five pounds.[99] There is no record to prove that Townsend was released but there is no reason why he should have been treated differently from his three fellow Chartists.

Trial[100]

The trial took place at the Monmouth Summer Assizes, held at the Shire Hall on Friday August 2nd, with Baron Alderson as the presiding judge. Fearing trouble, the authorities had stationed a contingent of Lancers at Coleford, five miles away in the Forest of Dean, 'so that their services could be obtained at a very short notice', and the Mayor of Monmouth had sworn in a number of special constables. It was a hot day, and by the time the proceedings began at nine thirty, the court room was 'crowded to suffocation'.[101]

The prosecution was led by Serjeant Talfourd, Radical MP for Reading from 1835-41, promoter of copyright law reform and friend of Charles Dickens, who dedicated *The Pickwick Papers* to Talfourd when it was first published in book form in 1837.

Shire Hall, Monmouth, 1860

The principal defence barrister was John Arthur Roebuck, another Radical MP, this time for Bath from 1832-37 and 1841-47, who had written the introduction to the version of the Charter published in 1838: he was known for his vehement debating style which earned him the nickname of 'Tear 'em' and embroiled him in at least one duel.[102]

The prisoners were charged with unlawful assembly and conspiracy, referring to meetings held at Pentonville in Newport on April 19th, and on five other dates in March and April. Other charges of a similar nature against Edwards, Vincent and John Frost relating to meetings in the Pontypool area were held over until the next assizes.

Alderson began by explaining the nature of the two alleged offences:

> *Any meeting assembled under such circumstances as, according to the opinion of rational and firm men, are likely to endanger the peace of the neighbourhood, or as would alarm persons of reasonable firmness and courage, is an unlawful assembly. The jury should take into consideration the way in which the meetings were held, the hour of the day, and the language used by the persons assembled and by those who addressed them.*

> *Criminal conspiracy consists either in combination and agreement to do an illegal act... or to effect a legal purpose by illegal means. Conspiracy to incite to disaffection is criminal; and so is the use or show of physical force; but petitioning to bring about an alteration of the law is not unlawful.*

Although the arrests had been made by order of the Newport magistrates, the cases were proceeding at the order and expense of the Government, which is an indication of the anxiety felt by the authorities at the deteriorating political situation. All four of the accused pleaded 'not guilty' to the charges 'in a very audible voice'. Their appearance was considered to be 'very respectable' by the correspondent of the *Hereford Journal*, who also noted that 'Edwards is a man of remarkable muscular proportions'.[103]

Talfourd then set out the case for the prosecution. He began by describing six Chartist meetings which had taken place in Newport between March 19th and April 26th, five of them in Pentonville and the sixth and last near the Bristol steam packet wharf on the east bank of the River Usk. Talfourd described Edwards as 'a person of considerable physical power', and highlighted his role in combing the town for supporters and leading them in noisy procession through the dark streets to the meeting site, with marchers arranged in ranks of five or six abreast, often with arms linked. Rule Britannia was sometimes sung, and the persons or homes of unpopular locals were hissed and hooted when encountered. Edwards was sometimes noted to be carrying a short stick, though he denied this,[104] as were a number of others. Talfourd suggested in summary that 'The aspect of these processions, which came after dark along the streets, was such as to excite terror and alarm among the peaceable inhabitants of the place'.

At the meetings themselves, Vincent was the principal speaker on every occasion. Townsend and Dickenson also sometimes either spoke or chaired the meetings, but Edwards's role seemed to be policing the crowd - he referred to some of his supporters as his 'special constables', and at the meeting on April 25th, according to Thomas Phillips, was heard to say 'Each of you must watch his neighbour'. On March 27th, in response to Vincent saying that every hill and valley would be prepared to send forth its army if required by the Convention, if the National Petition was rejected, 'Edwards held up an arm of considerable force, crying out at the same time "Here is stuff!"'

Talfourd's case against Vincent rested on his use of language, and he used a number of examples as evidence of his guilt. On March 27th, after denouncing Thomas Phillips and Thomas Prothero as two of the greatest enemies of the working man, Vincent said 'I should like to see Mr Prothero hung up to that lamp-post, and when he is cut down I could point out a fit place for his interment'. On April 18th, he told his audience, 'You are not bound by the laws, because they are made by men in the election of whom you have no voice'. Then on April 19th Vincent said, 'When the time for resistance arrives let the cry be "To your tents, O Israel" and then with one voice, one heart and one blow perish the privileged orders! Death to the aristocracy! Up with the people and the Government they have established'. At the riverside on

April 26th, having seen a member of the Christchurch Yeomanry riding past, he said to the crowd, 'What fists you have, what legs you have; and your shoes, how thick they are and what nails there are in them, and if by chance you should kick one of those fellows, what would become of him?'

When Talfourd concluded, he was applauded by the public onlookers, eliciting a rebuke from Alderson: 'I expect but perfect order and decorum'.

After Talfourd's opening speech, the prosecution called a number of witnesses to support the account he had given, including Thomas Phillips, Mayor of Newport; Morris Morris, shoemaker and former member of NWMA; Watkin Richards, the harbour-master; Thomas Hawkins, ironmonger; John Fraser, officer of the Monmouthshire and Glamorgan Banking Company; Thomas Phillpotts, solicitor, High Street; Henry Williams, surveyor, Pentonville; Isaiah Waterloo Nicholson Keyes, worker at the office of the *Monmouthshire Merlin*; Joseph Johnson, commercial traveller; and Edward Harris, master saddler. Most of them had either seen the crowds processing to the meetings, or attended the meetings themselves.

Roebuck mounted a robust defence, stating at the outset that the Newport meetings were similar in character to those which took place in the Reform campaign in the early 1830s, which had been supported by the Whigs, now the ruling party. He argued that mass meetings and the use of incendiary language were common features of many extra-parliamentary campaigns, including those opposed to the Corn Laws and in favour of the abolition of slavery, and also cited the example of Daniel O'Connell, a favourite of the Government, who had numerous armed followers in Ireland and had held many huge public meetings there. He said that the Newport meetings posed no danger and had not led to any breach of the peace, and that they were held at night so that working people could attend, noting that Parliament sat at night as well. Sticks were carried by a large section of the population, and it was common practice for marchers such as those in friendly society parades to link arms. He felt that Vincent's comments had been taken out of context, and that the witnesses had agreed that he had often urged peace and order in his addresses. Roebuck also made the point that public meetings were an important part of the constitution, as they provided a way for those without a vote to make their feelings known to Parliament.

His speech was followed by some applause and some hisses from the packed court room, again provoking the displeasure of Baron Alderson.

The jury took fifteen minutes to reach a decision: all four defendants were found guilty of attending illegal meetings; Vincent and Edwards were found guilty of using violent and seditious language; but all four were acquitted of conspiracy.

In sentencing, Alderson commented that Vincent would be dealt with more harshly as he was the ringleader, and had come to Newport from another area to agitate. He was sentenced to 12 months in gaol, Edwards to nine months and Dickenson and Townsend each to six months. The prisoners listened to the judge 'with great attention', and their demeanour was 'marked by propriety'.[105] The trial concluded at eight o'clock.

According to the *Merlin*, an immense crowd was waiting outside the Shire Hall as the prisoners were removed to the prison van, and a few cries of 'Vincent for ever' were heard. 'The vehicle went on quietly to its place of destination.'[106]

Monmouth Gaol

When the doors of Monmouth Gaol closed behind the convicted Chartists, they found that the conditions of their imprisonment had changed for the worse. Instead of enjoying the freedom to purchase their own food supplies they were now limited to the standard daily prison diet, which consisted of a pound and a half of bread at least 24 hours old, one pound of potatoes, and two quarts of gruel - considered to be 'pig's victuals' by Edwards.[107] This may have contributed to the only recorded sickness he experienced during his stay in Monmouth: a seven day period when he was 'ill... with haemorrhoids'.[108] Their access to books, pens, ink and paper was restricted, but they were still allowed to wear their own clothes, and they were not subjected to the unwanted attention of the prison barber.[109] Previously the punishment of political prisoners in Britain had been limited to the deprivation of their liberty alone, so the new restrictions outraged the four men and their supporters, but their regime remained preferable to that endured by common criminals: grey prison uniform, prison diet, prison haircut and sometimes hard labour.

On August 20th Edwards, Vincent and Dickenson wrote to Lord John Russell, the Home Secretary, complaining that they were deprived of writing materials, were not allowed the free use of books, and were restricted to prison rations. Their petition claimed that after sentencing them Baron Alderson had 'expressed a wish that we should be subject to no other inconvenience beyond that of imprisonment', and alleged that they had been treated 'with unprecedented rigour for offences of a Political nature'. They felt that the evidence against them had been 'weak and contradictory', and said that the principal witnesses against them had sworn that they had 'always inculcated obedience to the laws, preservation of the peace, and the protection of Life and Property at all those meetings, for attending which we are imprisoned'.[110]

The authorities at Monmouth must have been aware of the dissatisfaction felt by the Chartist prisoners: on August 11th Charles Marriott of Newton House, justice of the peace, one of the visiting justices responsible for the administration of Monmouth Gaol, former Sheriff of Monmouthshire, and one of the signatories of the *Rules, Orders, and Regulations for the Government of the Gaol of Monmouth*, published in 1832, wrote to Russell informing him of the precise conditions in which they were being confined. He explained the concessions which had been made to them in the matters of clothing and haircutting, stated that they had been permitted to write once to friends, and enclosed a copy of the *Rules* for Russell's information.[111]

On August 22nd Lord Brougham raised the question of the three Chartists' petition in the House of Lords. Brougham was a prominent supporter of Reform in the early 1830s and had been Lord Chancellor for four years in Lord Melbourne's Whig government: in addition to detailing the petitioners' complaints about the hardships of their confinement, he also questioned the validity of imprisoning them for attending the same type of meeting that was commonplace during the Reform campaign. Prime Minister Melbourne's response was that the prisoners 'were subjected to the same regulations as all other prisoners in the same ward... he did not see any reason why there should be any extraordinary interposition in favour of these petitioners'.[112]

Melbourne's comments notwithstanding, it appears that as a result of the prisoners' complaints and the representations on their behalf, Lord John Russell wrote to Marriott ordering him to allow them limited access to books, and there seems to have been some easing of the rules on correspondence, although they remained on the standard prison diet.[113] Despite this modest concession, they continued to be subjected to treatment which they considered to be unjust. In September Sarah

Edwards travelled 'all the way to Monmouth' but was denied access to her husband when she got there. An indignant editorial in the *Vindicator* sympathised: 'The feelings of this poor woman may be more easily felt than described... in what respect could a conference between Edwards and his wife have affected his safe detention?'[114] A further petition from the prisoners was submitted to the Monmouthshire magistrates in October, asking for the free use of books and writing materials and for permission to buy their own food. They made the point that the Attorney General had said that the only desire of the authorities was to hold them in safe custody, and not to keep them 'subject to the Diet and Regulations under which men labour *who have been guilty of the most serious offences*'. (Emphasis in the original.)[115]

On August 12th a Chartist meeting had been held at Dukestown in Breconshire, attended by 'upwards of 2500 people' according to a report in the *Merlin*, with Dr William Price in the chair. William Jones told the crowd that attempts would be made to get Vincent and his fellow prisoners out of gaol by fair means, 'but that they were determined to get them out at any rate'. John Frost also addressed the meeting, and a resolution was adopted authorising him to 'wait on Lord John Russell, and request his lordship to recommend the crown to remit the sentence of Vincent and his fellow prisoners'. The meeting closed with several rounds of cheers, including one for the Monmouth prisoners.[116] Frost did his best to carry out the wishes of the meeting, beginning on August 26th when he wrote to Russell requesting a meeting to discuss the cases of Vincent, Edwards, Townsend and Dickenson.[117] Russell refused, but promised that if Frost submitted a 'properly worded petition' he would present it to the Queen. Frost duly forwarded a copy of the resolution passed at Dukestown, but the reply from Samuel March Phillipps, Permanent Under-Secretary at the Home Office, on behalf of Lord Normanby, who had just replaced Russell as Home Secretary, dismissed the request. Normanby said that a resolution passed at a meeting could not be placed before the Queen, and added that even if the form and language had been appropriate, he still would not have brought it to her attention. Frost then changed tack, asking for a meeting with Normanby to discuss the treatment of political prisoners but this was again rejected, although Normanby agreed to consider a submission in writing. This was sent by Frost in a letter in which he asked for the prisoners to be given unrestricted access to writing materials, books and newspapers and unlimited visiting by relatives and friends 'at all reasonable hours'; to be allowed to stay out of their cells until nine p.m. in the winter and ten p.m. in the summer; to have the use of fire and candles in the evenings; and to be granted the right to buy food to supplement the prison diet. In his reply on behalf of Normanby, Fox Maule, Under-Secretary of State for the Home Department, said that the prisoners had already been allowed 'such indulgences as are consistent with the ends of justice and the regulations of the prison in which they are confined'. Frost was obviously exasperated by the continued rebuffs, and his final letter in the sequence, written on September 10th, made the case passionately and indignantly for the Chartists' sentences to be quashed, or failing that, for their conditions to be improved. Someone in the Home Office wrote 'He is an impudent fellow' on the outside of the letter.[118]

Frost, together with Zephaniah Williams, William Jones and other Chartists, was detained in Monmouth Gaol from his arrest on November 4th following the Newport Rising until his transfer on February 2nd to the prison hulk *York* in Portsmouth in readiness for transportation to Van Diemen's Land. On November 9th John Vaughan, one of the visiting justices, noted that the gaoler had been instructed to move Edwards, Vincent and Dickenson into the debtors' ward, 'in order the more effectively to prevent any communication (with) the prisoners committed for high treason'.[119] There is no record of any meeting between Edwards and Frost during the time that they were both in Monmouth, but in a letter dated February 15th 1840, Vincent mentioned a 'private meeting' that he had with Frost in the prison.[120] In the lead up to the trial of Frost, Jones and Williams, Edwards's brother-in-law - probably Mary Brewer's husband - was prosecuted for threatening potential jury members that they would 'have their guts cut out'.[121]

Townsend, who had been viewed more favourably by the prosecution than the other three because of his youth, had been freed early after serving a month of his sentence, but Dickenson remained at Monmouth for the full duration of his punishment and was released on January 31st 1840.[122]

Second Trial[123]

On March 30th 1840, Edwards and Vincent were brought before Baron Gurney and a Special Jury at the assizes at Monmouth Shire Hall for consideration of further charges of conspiracy and attending illegal meetings which had been held back from their original trial. The charges this time related to the meeting in Pontnewynydd on New Year's Day 1839, which chose John Frost as the delegate from Pontypool to the Chartist National Convention, and to several meetings in April in the Pontypool area, notable for Edwards's use of violent and colourful language. Frost was not present for obvious reasons: he had been found guilty of high treason for his part in the Newport Rising and was on his way to the penal colony in Van Diemen's Land on board the convict ship *Mandarin*.

Baron Gurney was considered to be an independent but harsh judge. He had prosecuted the Cato Street conspirators in 1820, and in 1835 he became the last judge in England to impose a capital punishment for sodomy. In 1843 he sentenced three Rebecca rioters to transportation. The prosecution was once again led by Serjeant Talfourd while Edwards was defended by Sir Codrington Edmund Carrington, who had been Tory MP for St Mawes from 1826-31.[124] Vincent had elected to conduct his own defence, having been unimpressed by Roebuck's presentation at the first trial in August, which he called 'a horrible thing; as cold as lead; and as formal as the devil'.[125] Frost had also criticised Roebuck for not calling witnesses for the defence in one of his letters to the Home Office in September 1839.

According to the *Northern Star*, 'very great excitement prevailed in Monmouth for many days' prior to the trial, and the court room was 'crowded to excess' when proceedings began at nine o'clock.

Talfourd started his presentation of the case for the prosecution by explaining that the two men were accused of 'conspiracy to effect great changes in the Government by illegal means, and also of unlawful assembly'. In his description of the Pontnewynydd meeting he stated that Edwards had said that he had a strong arm, that many lives would be lost for the cause, and that he was not afraid to lose his own. Talfourd said that on April 5th Edwards addressed the meeting 'in language which he hoped was without parallel, as it would be found that he used, with fearful force, the denunciation of Heaven's vengeance contained within the Old Testament'. Talfourd went on to discuss Vincent's speeches at the meetings, and quoted him as saying at Pontypool on April 24th, 'Will you act with the Convention in ulterior proceedings if the Charter is refused?', which was answered by a cry of 'We will' from the crowd.

The prosecution called witnesses who had attended the meetings and they gave accounts of what they had seen and heard. They included David Jones, a commercial agent of Pontypool; William Llewellyn, a civil engineer who lived near Pontypool; John Roberts, the superintendent of police at Pontypool; and George Essex, occupation unspecified.

Carrington's defence of Edwards was very similar to that used by Roebuck in the August trial. The meetings under consideration had all been peaceful, there had been no blows exchanged, and no broken windows, not even 'at the house of the most unpopular man in the district'. None of the witnesses had experienced any terror or alarm. He went on to compare the meetings with those held during the Reform campaign when very strong language had sometimes been used but no prosecutions had ensued: indeed he considered that the expressions attributed to Edwards were 'incidental words of the moment'. He questioned the accuracy of the evidence, emphasising how difficult it was for the witnesses to remember the content of speeches correctly after the event.

Vincent's defence speech lasted for two hours, and Gurney later complimented him 'on the ability he had displayed in his address to the jury'. In general he relied on the same arguments that Carrington had used. He complained that the extracts that had been quoted from his speeches were partial, and that it was well known that public speakers were often carried away by the excitement of the occasion. The Reform movement had utilised public meetings in the same way that the Chartists had done, and used similar rhetoric, without punishment. Vincent said that at the meetings he had counselled people to be 'sober, honest and orderly'.

In his summing up, Gurney made a statement full of significance in the light of the Newport Rising, which had taken place since Vincent and Edwards's first trial. 'The question was not whether there was any direct excitation to violence at the time of these meetings, but whether it was not intended that the people should be excited to disaffection, and kept quiet for a time, till it was thought fit that they should proceed to violence on a given signal.'

The jury took a mere ten minutes to come to a decision, and found both men guilty, although they 'recommended them to mercy on account of the long imprisonment they had undergone'.

Gurney considered that Edwards was the more culpable of the two, saying that the evidence against him was 'of the most flagrant description'. He sentenced Edwards to a further fourteen months in prison and Vincent to an extra twelve months, and the trial ended at six in the evening.

Millbank Penitentiary

Worried about the possibility of further popular unrest in the aftermath of the Newport Rising and the trial and transportation of Frost, Williams and Jones, both the visiting justices responsible for Monmouth Gaol and the Government decided that it was inadvisable for Edwards and Vincent to remain in Monmouth, where their presence could provide a focus for local agitation and protest. It was also noted that one of the objectives attributed to the Newport insurrectionists was the liberation of the Chartist prisoners held in Monmouth.[126]

County gaols were funded and administered locally, so it was not considered reasonable to request that the prisoners should be housed in a gaol in a distant part of the country where they would be a burden on the local taxpayers. The only option available was to move them to Millbank Penitentiary in London, a national institution run by the state.[127]

On Wednesday April 8th, Edwards and Vincent, together with another Chartist prisoner, William Shellard of Pontypool, left Monmouth chained together in the custody of the gaoler, arriving at Millbank at 10 o'clock the same night.[128]

The penitentiary was a forbidding hexagonal building with six petal shaped wings, sited on marshy ground in Westminster next to the River Thames. It had been completed in 1821 at a cost of £500,000, and was designed to hold just over a thousand male and female prisoners. It acted as a holding site for prisoners awaiting transportation, who made their exit from Britain along dank tunnels connecting the prison with the nearby Thames and the waiting convict ships, and it also housed prisoners convicted of criminal offences and others whose sentences of transportation had been commuted to imprisonment.[129] The regime was harsh: prison clothing was compulsory; inmates were housed in solitary cells, and were not permitted to speak to each other during exercise periods for the first half of their sentence; masks had to be worn during exercise; and labour, principally making shoes or mailbags, was compulsory. Sanitation and drainage were poor: the water supply was taken directly from the river, and although it was filtered, the prison suffered from outbreaks of cholera.[130] Vincent was compelled to work as a tailor,[131] and wrote of the 'smoky, stinking miasmas of Millbank'.[132]

On arrival the Chartist prisoners were ordered to strip and wash, and were then given prison uniform and told not to speak. The following morning Edwards had to scrub a long stone passage on his hands and knees, before being 'put to learn the trade of breeches-maker to the queen'. He found solitary confinement to be 'very injurious to my constitution'.[133]

Petitions were raised on behalf of the prisoners, asking that they should be returned to Monmouth. One from Birmingham was presented to Parliament on June 2nd by Serjeant Talfourd, the prosecutor of Edwards and Vincent in both of their trials. He argued that confinement in Millbank entailed a degree of punishment that was inappropriate for political offences, for which deprivation of personal liberty had previously been the sole penalty, and that incarceration in the Penitentiary had never been contemplated when the sentences were imposed. On behalf of the Government, both Fox Maule and Lord John Russell explained the background to the decision to move the prisoners, and refused to consider the possibility of returning them to Monmouth.[134] But a change of heart must have occurred in the days following the discussion in the House of Commons, as an order for the removal of Edwards, Vincent and Shellard from Millbank to the Rutland county gaol in Oakham was issued on June 5th.[135] Despite the rigours of the two months he spent in the Penitentiary, James Wade, the surgeon at Millbank, reported to the Governor of Oakham Gaol on July 2nd that 'Edwards enjoyed perfect health during that time, and left this institution free from any complaint'.[136]

Oakham Gaol

The prisoners were transferred from Millbank on June 9th on the Leeds mail coach, this time unchained,[137] and remained in their new gaol until their release in 1841.

Oakham was the county town of Rutland and lies about twenty five miles east of Leicester and a hundred miles north of London, sufficiently far from the scene of the Chartists' crimes for the authorities to feel confident that the prisoners would not provide a target for an attempt to release them by force. Initially they were treated in the same way as all 'misdemeanants' in Oakham except that they were allowed their own clothes and were placed in separate accommodation.[138] This meant that their conditions were very similar to those that they had been accustomed to in Monmouth: each of them had a sleeping cell with a wooden bedstead and 'ample bedding', and they had the exclusive use of a day room with a fireplace. Their diet remained the standard prison allowance with the addition of one and a half pounds of meat per week each, and they were allowed only religious books lent to them by the Chaplain. But the fact that in many ways they were still treated like convicted criminals rankled, and on June 17th Vincent wrote on behalf of all three of them to Normanby, requesting that they be allowed to purchase their own supplies, have access to a wider range of books, and be given knives and forks instead of the standard issue wooden spoons, which had forced them to eat with their hands. Vincent added that the Oakham diet was inferior to that at the Penitentiary and that they were all very weak, Shellard in particular.[139] Edwards, Vincent and Shellard sent separate individual petitions to Thomas Duncombe, the Radical MP for Finsbury with the same complaints, Edwards in addition bemoaning his 'lost health and strength'.[140] Normanby acted swiftly and all their requests were granted: by September Vincent was learning French and mentioned in a letter that they were to be allowed to stay out of their bed-cells until eight o'clock at night in the winter, rather than being locked up at the usual four o'clock.[141] There was a limit to the authorities' willingness to compromise, however, and the prisoners were not allowed to receive the *Northern Star*.[142] On July 3rd, William Orridge, the prison Governor wrote to Fox Maule that Edwards was in good health and added, 'I am not aware that he makes any complaint', contradicting the claims by Edwards in his recent petition.[143]

On July 10th the House of Commons debated a motion proposed by Duncombe, which called for the Government to legislate to ensure that the only punishment for those convicted of political offences, who were guilty of no moral crime, should be the deprivation of their liberty as had previously been the case. Duncombe said that

Thomas Duncombe MP

in the last twelve months there had been numerous instances where the punishment inflicted on political prisoners had been far harsher than the sentencing judge had intended, and cited Edwards and Vincent and their confinement in Millbank as examples. Among those supporting his motion were Serjeant Talfourd and Benjamin D'Israeli, but the Whig Government argued that the existing regulations allowed for prisoners to petition to have their conditions ameliorated and again referred to Edwards and Vincent and the prompt response to their Oakham complaints to show that the system worked: the proposal was defeated by 117 votes to 29.[144]

The months that he spent in gaol gave Edwards plenty of time to ponder his past conduct and future intentions, and in a letter to the *Northern Star* in November 1840, he wrote 'although my body has been bound in prisons and cells, yet my mind has been free and unshackled'. He believed that drunkenness was one of the causes of the oppression of the working classes, and pledged himself to teetotalism.[145] Vincent had given up alcohol in 1836, and wrote an address on temperance while in Oakham, which was signed by both Edwards and Shellard: it was published in the *Northern Star* and other newspapers in November 1840.[146]

In the same letter, Edwards stated 'When I leave this place I will take out a license to preach the glorious Gospel of the blessed God', and said that he would devote all his energies to the emancipation of his country. He promised to do anything he could to promote peace in Newport, and to improve 'its condition and the state of its inhabitants'. Intriguingly, he said that he had been in communication with 'gentlemen' who would provide him with a room when he was released where people could gather 'to promote their mental, moral, social and political improvement... I will rally the men of Newport around that moral and intellectual standard which the Chartists of Britain are now upraising'. He concluded, 'Those who wish to reform others should first reform themselves. This I have done, and I will take care to conduct myself in such a way as shall merit the approbation and support of all the wise and virtuous in Newport and its vicinity'.

In February and March 1841 Edwards wrote a series of five letters to the *Midland Counties Illuminator*, a Chartist newspaper published in Leicester, which appeared under the heading 'Letters from Oakham Gaol'. Edwards covered a wide range of topics including the importance of education and temperance in the Chartist movement, a discussion of tactics that should be used in the campaign for the Charter, and what the achievement of the Charter would mean, as well as describing his own experiences and the financial hardships that had resulted from his work for the cause.[147]

Undoubtedly Edwards' time in prison caused significant financial difficulties for him and his family, as was the case for many other Chartist prisoners. He had spent a considerable time away from his work when campaigning in 1839, and although he had received some expenses they had failed to reimburse his costs by some margin. He gave the example of his trip to London in May to deliver petition signatures, which left him out of pocket by three pounds.[148] When Edwards's shop was raided 'at a very late hour of the night' in December 1839 during his time in gaol while his wife was running his newspaper and bookselling business, publications worth twenty pounds were seized and were never returned.[149] It appears that this action by the authorities was illegal: Thomas Jones Phillips, clerk to the magistrates in Newport, described in two letters to Normanby how he had authorised the seizure after he heard that the *Western Vindicator* was 'exposed for sale in the shop window of the wife of William Edwards', but he admitted that this was done without obtaining a warrant from the magistrates. He justified this by saying that 'it was considered better to risk the consequences of a little irregularity than to fail in putting a stop to the publication of papers of such pernicious thinking'.[150] It must be remembered that Phillips was acting in the weeks following the shock of the Newport Rising. According to the terms of his father's will Edwards should have received £50 in May 1840, twelve months after his mother's death, but there is no mention of this in any of his surviving writing.[151] Perhaps his political beliefs and his gaol sentence caused the trustees, one of whom was local landowner William Curre of Itton Court, to withhold the payment. In July 1840, the *Northern Star* published a list of nearly one hundred Chartist prisoners, and that month one of the first acts of the newly formed National Charter Association was the creation of a National Victim Fund run by a committee which raised money and dispersed it to prisoners' families.[152] Receipts and payments were published in the *Northern Star*, and a sum of more than £400 was allocated during the next twelve months.[153] Sarah Edwards received two payments of one pound each from the fund, in December 1840 and January 1841.[154] Local Chartist branches also raised money and

Edwards received one sovereign while in Oakham from Charles Groves, secretary of the Newport branch of the NCA, and other localities subscribed another five pounds.[155] Groves also wrote to the *Northern Star* to say that he had no knowledge of the rumoured fraudulent collecting of money in Newport purportedly for Edwards's assistance.[156] In February 1841 William Shellard wrote to the *Midland Counties Illuminator* on Edwards's behalf to publicise his financial problems, claiming that 'he is destitute of money altogether', and that prisoners in Oakham needed to buy clothes, materials for washing and shaving, extra coals, and some food.[157] Shellard said that Edwards had been 'persecuted by the enemies of liberty', and in another letter Edwards complained that he had been doing 'good business as a baker and grocer' in Newport, but that once he had become involved in Chartism those opposed to his views had tried to ruin him.[158] Shellard pointed out that when Edwards was released from prison he faced a long journey home which would cost him three or four pounds: he had given a pound to his fellow prisoner but could not afford more, and he ended with a plea for donations from the readers of the *Illuminator*. A letter from John Markham, one of the leaders of the Leicester Chartists, appeared in the same issue of the newspaper. Markham was a Primitive Methodist preacher, which gave him more in common with Edwards than just their shared political beliefs.[159] He had visited Edwards in Oakham on at least two occasions, and had been alarmed by the deterioration in his condition. Markham pointed out that Edwards had played no part in the Newport Rising, and asked people to contribute food or money. The appeals bore fruit, and a further four pounds were donated in the next three weeks.[160] In a letter written to the *Illuminator* on March 12th, Edwards thanked 'Col. Thompson and the friends of liberty in Leicester and Nottingham' for their help, and said that he had enough money to pay for his coach fare home.[161]

Edwards's term of imprisonment was due to end on May 26th 1841 and Vincent's on March 26th, but Vincent's sentence was reduced by two months, and he was released on February 1st.[162] Both men had been required to provide security against their good behaviour for five years following the expiration of their terms in gaol for £500 personally with two additional amounts of £100 each from other guarantors, but before his release Vincent's amounts had been reduced to a personal sum of £100 and two further amounts of £50. The consideration shown to Vincent by the authorities triggered a flurry of petitions to Normanby in February asking that Edwards should be granted the same remission of sentence and reduction of security, as the two men had been convicted of the same offences: four of these letters are retained in the records of the Home Office. One petition is from Edwards's wife Sarah, who said that she and her children were 'suffering severely from poverty and want', and another was from Edwards himself, with very similar wording, saying that he was 'entirely ruined in circumstances' due to the 'great length of his sentence'. The two other petitions were both from Newport, one from John Phillips, a shoemaker of Market Street, and Jonah Williams, a tailor of Llanarth Street, members of the National Charter Association: the other has no signatures surviving on the document.[163] Normanby agreed to the petitioners' requests and Edwards was released from Oakham Gaol on March 22nd, on the same terms as Vincent.[164]

I went to prison a Chartist, and I shall leave the prison a more determined Chartist than ever was before.[165]

William Edwards

FREEDOM

When William Edwards stood outside Oakham Gaol on the day of his release he was 43 years of age, and his relief at the end of his prison sentence must have been tempered by the thought of the daunting trip of more than one hundred and fifty miles back to Monmouthshire and the uncertain future which lay ahead of him. First he travelled to Leicester, where on the afternoon of his release he and Vincent were given a hero's welcome at a tea meeting in the New Hall, attended by more than 250 people. A public meeting followed, chaired by John Markham, and Edwards was greeted by 'long continued cheering' when it was his turn to speak. He thanked the audience for their financial help and reiterated his dedication to the Charter. Gloves were presented to both men for them and their wives, the meeting ended with a rendition of 'God Save John Frost' sung to the tune of the national anthem, and, at Vincent's suggestion, a collection was made for Edwards at the doors. A second meeting took place at the same venue the next day, this time chaired by Thomas Cooper, with more than 500 people in the audience. Speeches were made by Vincent and Edwards once again, and on this occasion Edwards spoke about the importance of education, independent thinking, piety, teetotalism and the desirability of dealing with traders sympathetic to their cause. Stockings were presented to both speakers for their wives, and three cheers were given for 'Mrs Vincent and the Chartist women of England', Vincent and Edwards, Feargus O'Connor, and all Chartist prisoners.[166]

On the morning of Wednesday March 24th Edwards set off for Newport: his wife Sarah and his daughter Mary Ann were waiting for him at their shop in Commercial Street, where Sarah had continued to sell newspapers and periodicals during his absence. When Edwards arrived home he took up the trade once more, and continued as a bookseller and stationer for the remainder of his life, first at what became number

60 Commercial Street, and later at number 173. The Edwards family is recorded at (60) Commercial Street in the 1841 census, taken on June 6th, with his occupation listed as 'bookseller'.

Edwards was returning to a traumatised and deeply divided town. In the aftermath of the Rising a number of prominent local Chartists had been arrested by the authorities and there had been a permanent military presence. In these circumstances it would not have been surprising if Chartism had disappeared as an active movement in Newport, but this was certainly not the case. On a national level the need for an organisation to coordinate the campaign had resulted in the formation of the National Charter Association in Manchester in July 1840, with Feargus O'Connor's weekly newspaper the *Northern Star* acting as its mouthpiece. By 1842 the NCA had a membership of more than 50,000 in more than 400 localities, one of which was Newport where a branch was established in November 1840.[167] Edwards became a member when he returned home after his release from gaol.[168]

Edwards stuck to his plans to resume campaigning and little time elapsed before he reappeared in Newport public life. Lord Melbourne's Whig government was becoming increasingly fragile through the spring and early summer: their budget was defeated in May, a vote of no confidence was lost on June 4th, and the dissolution of Parliament was expected at any time.[169] Fifty four residents of Newport wrote to Thomas Hughes, the Mayor, requesting him to call a public meeting 'to discuss the conduct of the present Administration, and of our electoral representative' (Reginald Blewitt), and the meeting took place in the Police Office on Monday June 7th at six o'clock. A number of Tories were present, including Thomas Jones Phillips, but most of the speakers were well known Newport Chartists, amongst them Townsend, Dickenson, and William Edwards, 'our old friend' according to the *Northern Star*, who proposed the third resolution, 'That this meeting pledges itself to make use of all constitutional means to obtain a fair representation of all classes of people in the Commons House of Parliament'.[170] This was noticeably more moderate in tone than the rhetoric he was using before his imprisonment, and it was passed unanimously. The following evening Edwards welcomed Vincent to his home in Commercial Street, from where his young colleague addressed 'a large number of persons', detailing his plans to stand as a candidate for Banbury in the imminent election. Vincent had been on a short tour of South Wales, visiting Merthyr and Cardiff before coming to Newport. Presumably he stayed overnight with Edwards, before leaving for his intended constituency the next day.[171] Edwards's triumphant return to local politics was not to last however, and he soon became engulfed by the controversy surrounding his own involvement in the general election which took place later that summer..

Chartist Election Candidate 1841

One of the 'Aims and Rules' of the National Charter Association was that 'the People shall, wherever convenient and practicable, (bring) forward Chartist candidates at every election...' A number of Chartists stood in the 1841 and 1847 general elections but their only success came in the latter year when Feargus O'Connor won a seat in Nottingham.[172] Although their chance of winning was slim in most constituencies, by nominating candidates Chartists were able to take advantage of the opportunity to expound their views to a large audience on a public platform, and in some cases they withdrew after the show of hands at the hustings, rather than force a poll which they knew they could not win.

In the 1840s Newport was part of the Monmouth Boroughs parliamentary constituency, which it formed in combination with Usk and Monmouth. The sitting MP was Reginald Blewitt of Llantarnam Abbey, the Whig founder of the *Monmouthshire Merlin*, who was first elected in 1837.[173] In 1841 no Tory stood, and a week before the election the Newport Chartists met and decided to put forward a candidate. Subsequent events were confused and resulted in a fiasco at the hustings and bitter controversy within the Chartist camp afterwards. The indisputable facts are that at the hustings in Monmouth Shire Hall on Wednesday 30th June, William Edwards, accompanied by his friend and fellow ex-prisoner John Dickenson, was proposed as a Chartist candidate by watchmaker John Buttery of Agincourt Square and seconded by Thomas Tyler, a whitesmith of Monnow Street, referred to patronisingly by *The Silurian* as 'a Chartist son of Vulcan'.[174] Blewitt was also proposed and seconded by the Whigs. Twenty minutes after the Hall opened, William Cronin, the secretary of the Newport branch of the NCA, announced the arrival of Dr William Price of Llantrisant, and an attempt was made by William Townsend to nominate him also as a Chartist candidate, but a proposer and seconder who were suitably qualified could not be found. Edwards did not withdraw, and there were no other candidates. After speeches by both Blewitt and Edwards a show of hands was called for by the Mayor of Monmouth, which Edwards won by a large margin. He then addressed the crowd saying that he had upheld the principles of democracy and achieved a glorious victory but that he withdrew from the poll because he wished to cause no further inconvenience and expense to Blewitt and because he was not qualified by law to become an MP. Buttery insisted that a poll should take place, the Mayor declared that it would open the next morning at eight o'clock, and Blewitt went on to win by 476 votes to nil.[175]

There seemed to be a strong feeling among the Newport Chartists that they had been betrayed by Edwards's unwillingness to stand aside for Dr Price and his refusal to contest the election after winning the show of hands, and violence erupted on the day of the poll. A crowd gathered in front of the Westgate Inn at midday, and and by the evening about a thousand people were present. On his return from Monmouth, delayed due to his overindulgence in alcohol the previous day according to the *Merlin*, who called him 'the anti-Teetotal Deputy-Attorney', Townsend addressed the crowd, allegedly saying 'You know where stones are to be found. You know how to use them'. Effigies of Edwards and Dickenson, made by 'denizens of the Friars' Fields', were flogged, hanged and burned and the mob, led by a drummer, paraded through the streets and proceeded to stone the houses of both men, causing considerable damage. Dickenson's home and shop stood opposite to the Westgate Inn, and all the front windows and shutters were destroyed: stones weighing several pounds each were found inside the building afterwards. Dickenson escaped through a rear door and sought refuge with a friend in nearby Skinner Street. The police had decided not to intervene, 'deeming it imprudent to act against such excited rioters'. Blewitt appealed for calm but was struck on the head by a stone, and order was only restored when a detachment of the Rifle Brigade cleared the streets in the early hours of the morning.[176] The degree of anger caused amongst the Newport Chartists by the events at Monmouth is apparent when the background of their two victims is considered: Edwards, the tireless worker for the Chartist cause, gaoled for his efforts; and Dickenson, the veteran radical who had been wounded at Peterloo.[177]

On July 2nd Townsend was brought before the Newport magistrates and was committed for trial at the next assizes on charges of riot and incitement to riot. He was released on bail of £200, half of this sum to be guaranteed personally and the remainder consisting of two sureties of £50 each from James Horner and Benjamin Francis, both prominent local Chartists.

Three aspects of the affair caused controversy and much debate among the local Chartists in the aftermath of the election: the legitimacy of Edwards's candidature; the tactics pursued at the hustings; and the question of whether or not Edwards was bribed by Blewitt or his supporters.

Edwards had excellent credentials to be considered as a potential candidate, with his record as a Chartist campaigner and his status as a recently released prisoner who had suffered for the cause. On 22nd June the Newport Chartists met to choose someone to contest the forthcoming election and Edwards and his opponents gave differing accounts of what took place. In a letter to the *Merlin*, Edwards maintained that he was chosen unanimously 'to bring the principles of the People's Charter before the public, to try to get a show of hands in favour of those principles' though not to go to the poll; that at the end of the meeting Dr William Price of Llantrisant was proposed and seconded as a candidate, and that he, Edwards, stated that while he would not support Price due to the doctor's advocacy of physical force, he would stand down if the doctor reached Monmouth in time for the hustings; and that on the morning of the day of nomination, the secretary of the Newport Chartists visited Edwards at his inn to show him a letter from Price saying that he could not be in Monmouth.[178] The following week the *Merlin* published a letter from William Cronin stating that Price, not Edwards, had been their unanimous choice as candidate, that Edwards had agreed to propose him, and that Edwards himself agreed that he would only stand if Price was unable or unwilling to help. Dr Price had written to Cronin expressing his willingness to stand and this letter had been shown to Edwards. The secretary felt that from that moment 'ambition laid hold of Edwards'. Cronin also expressed surprise that Edwards claimed to have qualms about Price's views as 'there was no man more loud in his demand for physical and brute force than you have been'.[179] It appears from Cronin's account and that of Jonah Williams, whose letter was printed in the *Northern Star* on 24th July, that rather than waiting for Price, Edwards set off for Monmouth with Dickenson on the evening before the hustings and misled the Monmouth Chartists into thinking that he was the first choice as candidate of the Newport branch. When Price arrived at the Shire Hall the next day, just after Edwards had been nominated, the Newport man refused to withdraw.[180]

There does not appear to have been any general agreement in the Chartist movement about the tactics they should pursue after a show of hands at the hustings. In some parts of the country their candidates took part in the subsequent poll, but it is notable that the only other Chartist to stand in Wales in the 1841 election was Morgan Williams of Merthyr Tydfil who easily defeated his opponent, Sir Josiah John Guest, on a hand count but who then, like Edwards, withdrew before the poll.[181] This course of action was justified on the basis that so few Chartists were entitled to vote that participation in the poll was futile, and Edwards maintained that he had always intended to withdraw after the show of hands and had clearly expressed this intention.[182] But John Buttery, Edwards's proposer, appeared to be angered by his action and it was he who insisted on the contest going to the poll.[183]

After the election there was a strong belief amongst both the Monmouth and Newport Chartists that Edwards had been bribed by Blewitt. William Cronin observed that Edwards had called at Blewitt's bank before setting off for Monmouth, and William Townsend hinted heavily at bribery in a letter to the *Merlin*.[184] Jonah Williams described how he found Dickenson drinking in Monmouth with Ebenezer Rogers, a strong supporter of Blewitt, who found it necessary to deny an accusation by the editor of the *Monmouthshire Advertiser* that he had been the agent responsible for bribing Edwards.[185] John Buttery claimed that Edwards came to his home and offered him money if he would consent to withdraw before polling.[186] In separate letters to the *Merlin* Edwards denied accepting any bribes or offering money to Buttery.[187] However Edwards was undoubtedly hard-pressed financially after his time in prison and may have been vulnerable to temptation. In his hustings speech he alluded to the fact that he had received no expenses to pay for his journey back to Newport after his release from Oakham, and Blewitt immediately intervened to say that he would try to help. On July 5th, he wrote to Normanby asking for '£5 to £10' to be paid to Edwards as it was intended that his sentence should be served in Monmouth Gaol, but the Government had moved him far away from his home causing him unnecessary expense: Normanby approved the grant.[188] Edwards had omitted to mention that Colonel Peronet Thompson and others had responded to the appeal by the *Midland Counties Illuminator* by subscribing enough money to pay for his coach fare back to Newport: maybe he felt that he was due the money from official sources. Edwards also made a formal application at the Police Court 'for the cost of repairs rendered necessary by the ruffianly attack' on July 1st.[189]

The *Merlin* gleefully plunged into the dispute on Edwards's behalf, conveniently forgetting all their past 'mad baker' insults and instead shamelessly praising the 'very temperate and, as it appeared to us, fairly reasoned' arguments set out in his letter to the paper, published on July 10th, and condemning the 'personal and violent' language of the responses from Cronin and Buttery which appeared in the paper the following week. They likened the fate of Edwards to that of Actaeon from Greek mythology, a hunter who was torn apart by his own hounds after he was transformed into a stag. Of course the *Merlin*, which supported Blewitt, was more than happy to see the Newport Chartists arguing amongst themselves and did everything possible to fan the flames. The same issue of the newspaper carried a letter of support for Edwards from his old acquaintance John Markham, the Leicester Chartist, who said 'That Edwards would sell the Chartist cause appears to me, after all his sufferings for, and devotedness to, its interests, utterly impossible'. Edwards's covering letter complained that the *Northern Star* had published a report of the election which was 'false... in every important particular', and he concluded with the Latin maxim '*audi alteram partem*', an invocation to listen to the other side.[190]

The matter was resolved on August 10th when Edwards appeared before a special council of twenty one members of the Newport branch of the NCA, at Jonah Williams's house in Llanarth Street. Benjamin Francis was in the chair, and three charges were made against Edwards: acting in coalition with the Whigs, accepting bribes, and insulting Feargus O'Connor. After the evidence for the first charge was presented by Cronin and W. James, Edwards said, 'Every word that Mr Cronin said is true. I own that I have acted wrong, and it was nothing but ambition that led me to do it'. He left the meeting before all the evidence for the charge of bribery had been outlined, and was found guilty on all three counts by the council. Dickenson, who did not attend, was also found guilty of the same charges and the council 'warned the country to beware of Edwards and Dickenson, let them go where they will.'[191]

Aftermath: bookseller and radical 1841-1849

It might have been expected after the fiasco of the 1841 Monmouth Boroughs election and his subsequent violent public humiliation in Newport, not to mention his pariah status in the eyes of the local branch of the NCA, that Edwards would withdraw from any public involvement in radical politics and the campaign for parliamentary reform. But evidence suggests that he was tougher than that: he continued to run his bookselling and newspaper business from the same premises that were wrecked by the mob, and an examination of the *Monmouthshire Merlin*, the *Northern Star* and other newspapers shows that he was an active campaigner for the Charter throughout the 1840s.

A public meeting was held on Friday November 19th 1841 at the Police Court in Commercial Street opposite St Paul's Church,[192] to draft a loyal address to be sent to Queen Victoria congratulating her on the birth of her first son. The meeting was hijacked by Newport Chartists - which the *Northern Star* called a 'Great and Glorious Victory of the Blistered Hands over the Broad Cloth Gentry' - and William Cronin proposed an addition to the original motion, which 'contained the usual quantum of adulation and flattery with which our Liege Lady the Queen has been so pestered'. The amendment drew Victoria's attention to the poverty and misery of the working classes, and asked for pardons for Frost, Williams and Jones. Edwards spoke in support of the addition, and concluded by wishing the Queen happiness during her life, 'but at its close he hoped Monarchical Government would be closed for ever'. William Townsend addressed the meeting just before Edwards, though it is not clear whether this was the former Chartist prisoner or his father, a Newport councillor. Edwards praised Townsend's words, and it is remarkable that he should appear in a public arena speaking alongside one and possibly two of the people most opposed to him in the acrimonious events earlier that year.[193]

On December 10th 1841 *The Welshman* published a copy of a letter sent by Edwards to the Merlin clarifying his position and that of the Chartists who attended the meeting on November 19th. He said that they would have been guilty of hypocrisy if they had congratulated the Queen but failed to remind her of the 'awful state... (of) hundreds of thousands of her subjects'. He also reiterated his view that the Monarchy should end with the Queen's death, and denied that he himself had joined in the congratulations on the birth of her son, saying, 'If half the nation run mad with joy because they are likely to have more taxes to pay, I will not do so'.[194]

Edwards was present at a meeting held on December 3rd to elect a new town councillor. According to the report in the *Glamorgan, Monmouth and Brecon Gazette and Merthyr Guardian*, after the candidates had addressed the electors at the close of the poll, 'Edwards, the Chartist spouter, also spoke at some length', claiming that Edward Thomas, the winner of the election, and the Mayor, Lewis Edwards, were both Chartists.[195] Thomas certainly was: as we have seen, he was treasurer of Newport WMA in 1839, a friend of Henry Vincent, and he chaired or spoke at many Chartist meetings, but Edwards was stretching reality in claiming his namesake Lewis as a radical.

Edwards's name appeared as one of the signatories of a notice dated December 9th 1841, requesting the Mayor of Newport to call a public meeting to petition the Queen to pardon Frost, Williams and Jones,[196] organised because the November 19th meeting had broken up without agreeing on a resolution, and Edward Thomas, the successful candidate in the December 3rd council election also signed. The meeting took place on Monday December 13th at the Police Court and was attended by more than 400 people. Edwards spoke at length and seconded the resolution. He reflected on his time in gaol, calling Monmouth under Charles Ford 'the worst prison in England', and admitted that he may have done wrong and been violent in the past, but promised 'I shall be more prudent for the future'. He reaffirmed his commitment to working for universal suffrage and the Charter for the rest of his days by legal, peaceful and constitutional means. He condemned the Rising, saying, 'It was said by the men of the north to the Convention, that when the National Petition should be presented to the House of Commons, behind every signature there should be a pike, behind every pike a dagger, and behind every dagger a musket; but we have lived to see the folly of this. The unfortunate insurrection of November 1839 was a God-send to the oppressors... Let us proceed peaceably, my friends...' In calling for the release of Frost, Williams and Jones he lavished praise on Frost's life and character, and said that the authorities should take their lead from the example of God's mercy. The next speaker after Edwards was William Cronin, his erstwhile nemesis, who proposed the second resolution.[197]

Further evidence of Edwards's reacceptance by the Chartist movement is provided by his appearance at a number of meetings in Abergavenny. On Wednesday 26th January 1842, Edwards seconded a motion to adopt the new National Petition at a meeting of the Abergavenny Chartists.[198] On Wednesday 16th March he spoke at another Chartist meeting in the town, and the following day he 'lectured for upwards of two hours on the principles of the Charter and the beneficial results that would flow from its becoming the law of the land'.[199] The *Northern Star* of 23rd April advertised that Edwards would lecture at the Chartist Association Room in Frogmore Street, Abergavenny on Tuesday 3rd May, and on May 7th the *Merlin* printed a report of the meeting 'from our correspondent', who confessed that he had never previously witnessed a Chartist event. The attendance of 80-90 was apparently far larger than usual which he attributed to the presence of Edwards as the guest speaker. After a couple of initial derogatory remarks - 'it was evident that education had not done much for him', 'his language was occasionally very coarse' - the account was positive. The reporter praised Edwards's 'great natural abilities', and recognised that 'the last few years of his life have proved, that having adopted certain principles, he has firmness enough to manfully promulgate them, and fearlessly to stand by them. In advocating the cause of Chartism... he displayed a considerable degree of talent...' After outlining the Six Points, and denouncing both Whigs and Tories, Edwards went on to 'dilate on the horrors of war... especially the injustice which led to the Afghanistan slaughter'.[200] In doing so, the report continued, Edwards 'gave utterance to sentiments of the most exalted philanthropy... that would have done credit to a Penn or a Wilberforce'. The speech ended with a plea for the importance of education in the achievement of good government, which could only be obtained by moral means. Most of this cast Edwards in a good light, and was a far cry from the days of the *Merlin's* depictions of him as a mad demagogue.[201]

Edwards was one of the signatories of a notice requesting the Mayor of Newport to call a public meeting on March 29th 1848 to discuss petitioning parliament to adopt the People's Charter. The meeting duly took place at the Old Bush Inn in Commercial

Street. Edwards 'was recognised as their "old tried friend" by the meeting', and seconded the petition. He 'pointed with some warmth to the great progress of Liberty on the Continent; and augered therefrom that the days of tyranny were doomed all over the world'.[202] On 17th June 1848 the *Cardiff and Merthyr Guardian* reported on 'a large Reform meeting' which had taken place in the Town Hall: Edwards was one of the speakers, and so was Reginald Blewitt.

Bereavement

Personal tragedy struck on November 14th 1842 when Sarah, his wife of more than twenty years who had supported him through his period of intense campaigning and his gaol sentence, died at home at the age of 46 from nervous debility with Edwards in attendance.[203] The condition has no exact modern equivalent, but was characterised by severe anxiety or depression, chronic fatigue and an inability to function, which makes it possible that the stress of Sarah's last few years contributed to her demise.[204] This was certainly the opinion of the author of a paragraph announcing her death which appeared in the *Merlin*, who wrote, 'Having for a few years undergone great mental anguish arising from the trials and sufferings of her husband, reason sank under the weight of her afflictions'. The writer went on to say that she died peacefully, surrounded by her family.[205]

Edwards was not to remain a widower for long, and on August 1st 1843 he married Ann Eliza Williams of Chepstow in the Priory Church of St Mary. There was a significant age difference: William was 46 but Ann was only nineteen, although she was recorded as being 'of full age' (over twenty one) on the marriage register. Ann's father, Theophilus Williams was a glazier, and it is likely that her parents were the witnesses.[206] It is possible that the couple met through Edwards's family connections in the Chepstow area. After the wedding he continued to live in Commercial Street in Newport with his new bride, where Ann helped to run the business.

It appears that Ann had already had a child before she married Edwards. Her son Theophilus was eight on March 31st 1851, the day of the census, so he must have been born between April 1st 1842 and March 31st 1843. Either he was the child of another father, or the relationship between Ann and William began before the death of Edwards's first wife. They had two more children, Ann Eliza and Augusta, born in 1847 and 1848. In 1847 Ann Edwards, stationer, of Commercial Street, was listed as a shareholder of the Chartist National Land Company.

Throughout the 1840s Edwards continued in the business of selling books, newspapers, periodicals and stationery, initially from his shop at 60 Commercial Street. In July 1844 Edwards moved his home and business to 173 Commercial Street, several doors away from the Westgate Inn, and next door but one to the drapery business of Edward Thomas, his old Chartist ally: an auction of his entire stock was advertised in the *Merlin* and it took place on the premises before the move. The goods included 'sundry stationery and about 3,000 volumes of books comprising theological, biographical, historical, and topographical works, romances and novels'.[207] This certainly amounts to a substantial stock, but some radical booksellers ran much bigger establishments: William Willis claimed to have more than 50,000 volumes at his shop in Hanging Ditch, Manchester.[208] Among the titles mentioned in the notice were the works of Shakespeare, James Fenimore Cooper's novels, Benjamin Franklin's *Life and Essays*, Volney's *Ruins of Empire*, *Robinson Crusoe* and Goldsmith's *Essays and Poems*. Volney was a freethinking French philosopher and historian who became secretary of the National Assembly after the Revolution: he was often toasted at Chartist gatherings alongside other members of the 'pantheon' such as Paine, Cartwright, Cobbett and Voltaire.[209] The advertisement stated that 'The whole of the stock in trade will be sold without reserve' as an entire new stock was being purchased for the new premises.[210] *Pigot's 1844 Directory of Monmouthshire* lists 'Brown and Edwards (periodical)' as booksellers in Commercial Street, so it is possible that the move to number 173 coincided with Edwards entering a new business partnership, but by 1847 when Edwards advertised in J. M. Scott's *Ancient and Modern History of Newport*, Brown was no longer involved. A Robert Brown, who lived in Gold Tops, who was possibly the Chartist poet 'Iota', was a member of the NCA and a shareholder in the National Land Company, but the surname is too common to conclude that this was the man who briefly went into business with Edwards. By 1847 Robert Brown was employed as a labourer.[211] It appears that Edwards's precarious finances persisted through the 1840s as another auction took place on February 19th 1845 at 173 Commercial Street when all of his stock-in-trade, furniture and effects

Commercial Street, Newport, circa 1860.
Edwards's shop at number 173 was in the second building from the left.

were sold 'for the benefit of creditors'. But Edwards continued in business from the same address, as evidenced by the 1847 advertisement mentioned above, although by then he was operating as a fruiterer as well as a stationer and bookseller.[212]

Edwards appeared sporadically in the columns of the *Merlin* and other South Wales newspapers during the 1840s for reasons not directly related to his advocacy of the Charter.

Newport Mechanics Institute had been established in 1841 with the support of William Townsend senior amongst others, with the intention of providing the means for 'mechanics' or manual labourers to better themselves by attending classes and lectures and using the reading room and library. Initially it operated from rooms in the Police Court, then moved to the new Town Hall in 1842 before acquiring purpose built accommodation in Dock Street in the 1850s. In November 1841 the *Glamorgan, Monmouth and Brecon Gazette and Merthyr Guardian* published an account of a meeting held to elect the committee of the Institute and William Edwards was one of the successful candidates. The list of members makes for interesting reading: among Edwards's colleagues on the committee were Reginald Blewitt's nephew Edward Dowling, the Editor and proprietor of the *Merlin*; and John O'Dwyer, a journalist on the paper and a printer, who in 1840 produced Dowling's scathing critique of the events of 1839, *The Rise and Fall of Chartism in Monmouthshire*, the first book published on the Newport Rising. Other members included Thomas Jones Phillips who arrested John Frost after the Rising, the Rev. James Francis, who preached the anti-Chartist sermon at St Pauls Church in Commercial Street in April 1839, and Thomas Richards, from the opposing political camp, who signed the notice requesting the Mayor to convene a public meeting to discuss the People's Charter in March 1848.[213] The first annual general meeting of the Institute took place in April 1842, and the report noted that William Edwards and William Loder, also a bookseller with premises at 83 Commercial Street, were appointed librarians: Edwards's name does not appear in the list of committee members in this report and it is probable that his new position meant that he had had to stand down.[214] His appointment lasted at least until mid 1843 as a report in the *Merlin* on May 6th of that year mentioned 'Mr W. Edwards, one of the librarians' notifying the Committee of the Institute that a complete set of the *Mechanics Magazine* had been presented by Thomas Hawkins,

Town Hall, Newport, 1843

one of the magistrates. The same report mentioned that Edwards was a member of a deputation appointed to 'solicit gifts of books etc. from the friends of education', and amongst the others in that party was J. M. Scott.[215] In 1842 Edwards himself donated books to the Institute library: gifts of Cobbett's *History of the Reformation* and of three volumes of the *Magazine of Science* were recorded in the *Merlin*.[216] There is no mention of Edwards in the manuscript minutes of the Newport Mechanics Institute Committee: the first surviving entry dates from October 31st 1843 so it is likely that he relinquished his position during that summer, perhaps due to his re-marriage in August.[217] Although he was well qualified for the post by virtue of his experience as a bookseller, it must have placed great demands on his time and energy: the Regulations of Newport Mechanics Institute, printed in 1842, specified that the library and reading room should be open from seven in the morning until ten at night in the summer, and from nine in the morning until ten at night in the winter.[218] It is possible that Edwards's involvement with the Mechanics Institute represented the realisation of the plans he mentioned in his letter to the *Northern Star* from Oakham Gaol on November 28th 1840.

It is apparent that Edwards's commitment to teetotalism which began in Oakham Gaol, was serious and sustained. On April 1st 1843, the *Merlin* reported on a meeting of Newport Teetotal Society which had taken place in the Town Hall the previous week, with 'Mr Edwards, bookseller, in the chair'. He introduced the guest speaker, Dr Reynolds of Abergavenny, 'in appropriate terms', and Reynolds proceeded to detail 'the frightful ravages made by intemperance on the constitution and well being of man'.[219] On July 22nd of the same year the *Merlin* carried a letter from Edwards describing how a teetotal meeting he had attended on the Green in Caerleon had been interrupted by a drunken 'bloated maltster, blowing like a porpoise', showing that he retained his liking for a colourful turn of phrase. He went on to describe his outrage that amongst other things, the maltster accused him of 'courting a young lady': this was less than a month before his marriage to the teenaged Ann Eliza! 'Julius of Caerleon' was provoked into a response, published in the *Merlin* on August 5th, in which he defended the character and conduct of the 'highly respected' maltster and declared his belief that 'lectures on teetotalism will be much "more honoured in the breach than the observance" if such orators as Mr E has proved himself are to be the promulgators of its doctrines'.[220]

Edwards attended a meeting at the Town Hall in April 1843 which had been called to support a petition demanding the deletion of the Educational Clauses from Sir James Graham's Factory Bill. This appears to be a strange cause for a Chartist to support, but the proposed factory schools were to be run by the Church of England: this was perceived as a deliberate attack on dissent and it provoked vehement opposition from many non-conformists. Edwards asked the meeting whether women were to be allowed to sign, and when answered in the negative, he 'proceeded in a long speech to advocate the necessity of a "female petition", which we understand was agreed to'.[221] At a second meeting for the same purpose held in May, Edwards at one point came forward and asked leave to support the resolution, but when allowed to do so, 'he proceeded in a somewhat irrelevant manner to declaim in favour of the People's Charter in general, and of Universal Suffrage in particular'.[222]

The prevention of an attempted burglary at 'the house of Miss Edwards, bookseller, Commercial Street' was reported by the *Merlin* on May 1st 1847. The apprehended man was 'Patrick Sullivan, one of the destitute Irish'. Refugees from the Great Famine were arriving in Newport in large numbers from early 1847, and by late February the streets were 'crowded with famishing and half-naked strangers'. Presumably Sullivan was one of these unfortunate people.[223]

On 17th May 1849 Edwards appeared before the Newport magistrates charged with the sale of *Sam Sly*, 'a scandalous and libellous publication'. *Sam Sly* was a scurrilous and gossipy magazine published by William Caffyn, a bookseller from London. Caffyn's shop contained a box in which anonymous contributions to the magazine could be posted, and just prior to Edwards's court appearance, he had been charged with the libel of the Vicar of Barking, who was alleged to have had an affair with his maid. Caffyn pleaded guilty and was imprisoned for six months.[224] In its report of Edwards's case the *Merlin* spluttered its moral outrage: 'A low, scurrilous and venomous publication, known by the name of *Sam Sly*, has recently so foully aspersed the character and disturbed the happiness of many amiable and virtuous family circles in Newport, by the malicious scribblings of unmanly and impure literary assassins, that the authorities considered it high time to put a stop to such scandalous proceedings, by suppressing the sale of the publication'. On behalf of the magistrates, the Mayor proposed to Edwards that 'if he would promise to sell no more numbers of this disgusting publication' the proceedings would be abandoned. True to character, Edwards tried to bargain with the bench, asking initially to be allowed to sell the sovereign's worth of copies which he had just ordered and paid for, and when that was refused, he wished to be permitted to sell the remaining copies left in his shop. After the magistrates told him that he could use those to light his fire instead, he eventually agreed to comply with their request and was discharged: it is notable that the report referred to Edwards's age (52) and 'physical infirmities'.[225] From this and other sources we can build up a picture of the type of magazine or periodical sold by Edwards. In the raid on his shop on December 7th 1839 while he was in gaol, copies of the *Western Vindicator*, the *Penny Satirist*, *Figaro* and *The Bristol Spy* were seized.[226] An advertisement in the *Bristol Times* on May 4th 1839 for G. Payne, printer and publisher of the *Western Vindicato*r and wholesale distributor of newspapers and periodicals, mentions W. Edwards of Newport as an agent for the sale of publications listed in the notice: these included the *Northern Star*, *The Charter*, *The Chartist* and *Cleave's Penny Gazette*. As we have seen, *Sam Sly* carried scandalous features on the private lives of notable people, while *Figaro* and the *Penny Satirist* were radically oriented satirical journals and *Cleave's Penny Gazette* was owned by John Cleave, Chartist and member of the London Working Men's Association.

Edwards's poor health was apparent when he appeared before the magistrates in May, and on July 8th he died at his home in Commercial Street, attended by William Lewis of Canal Parade. The causes of death were *pthisis pulmonalis* (tuberculosis), from which he had suffered for nine months; and colliquative diarrhoea for six weeks.[227] The latter is diarrhoea associated with an excessive discharge of fluid, which is the principal symptom of cholera. There was an outbreak in Newport in mid 1849 which caused more than two hundred deaths, but the duration of his symptoms and the fact that cholera was not mentioned on his death certificate make it unlikely that Edwards was one of the victims. Tuberculosis was responsible for around a third of all deaths in the first half of the 19th century.[228] The death was recorded by William Downing Evans, an accomplished poet, composer and artist who was the registrar of births, marriages and deaths in Newport for more than fifty years from 1837. Edwards's old enemy, the *Merlin*, reported his demise on the 21st July: 'the bookseller, who had for many years been a determined supporter of Chartist opinions in Newport and elsewhere, a few days since breathed his last after a painful illness'. The paper reported that Edwards's sister-in-law, who was also living in 173 Commercial Street, heard at the same time of the death of her husband in America, leaving 'two young sisters and mothers... widows under the same roof'.[229] A paragraph noting Edwards's death also appeared in the *Leicestershire Mercury*, probably written by John Markham. The report claimed that Edwards's health had been poor since his release from gaol in 1841, and that he attributed this to 'sleeping in a bed that was much too short for him, he being a very tall and stout man, so that his feet were frequently exposed to the cold air of the prison'. The writer had last seen Edwards in 1848, when he was 'very emaciated... a mere skeleton of skin and bones'.[230]

It has not been possible to establish where Edwards was buried. There were two Independent chapels in Newport at the time of his death.[231] There are no surviving records for burials at Mill Street Chapel for 1849 beyond January,[232] and Tabernacle Chapel in Commercial Street stopped recording details of burials there after 1842 as it was felt that this was duplicating the work of civil death registration which had started in 1837. There is a note in the Tabernacle records to say that 'Three hundred corpses were buried in the Chapel yard' between 1842 and 1854 when the yard closed, 'most of them children'.[233] It is likely that Edwards was interred at one of these two graveyards, but both burial sites have been obliterated by urban redevelopment.

Edwards's widow and her three children were recorded in the 1851 census for Newport, collected on March 31st, still living at 173 Commercial Street, and it appears that Ann was continuing to run the bookselling business. Her widowed sister and son had remained with her, and her 74 year old mother, Ann, now widowed, had also moved in. The household was augmented by a female servant and a nursemaid aged 15 and 13 respectively, and a 33 year old woman visiting from Chepstow, making ten residents in all. In 1860 Ann, her sister and their children emigrated to Wisconsin. [234]

Having adopted certain principles, he has firmness enough to manfully promulgate them, and fearlessly to stand by them.[235]

Monmouthshire Merlin

MAD BAKER OR MAN OF PRINCIPLE?

William Edwards lived through a stormy period of British history. He was born just seven years after the French Revolution and was initially radicalised by two of its consequences - the Napoleonic Wars and their after-effects, and the reluctance of the British authorities to respond to demands for political change. Rapid industrialisation was changing the face of the country: Edwards was caught up in the migration from the countryside to the expanding towns, and in Newport he witnessed the growth of a booming port at first hand. The Peterloo massacre, the campaign for parliamentary reform, the introduction of the New Poor Law, epidemics of cholera and the Irish famine all occurred during his lifetime and influenced him, but the growth of Chartism from 1838 captured his imagination and gave him the opportunity to channel his passion and energy into a movement which appeared to have a chance of achieving aims in which he had long believed.

To some extent Edwards's role in the story of South Wales Chartism has been underestimated, perhaps because he took no part in the Newport Rising, but there is little doubt that he was one of the movement's most significant figures. Ivor Wilks concluded that only Zephaniah Williams and William Jones 'might claim comparable standing'.[236] His surviving writing reveals that he was far from the ludicrous figure of fun portrayed in the Whig and Tory newspapers: his letters and articles are well written, and he shows a knowledge of history and an ability to quote figures from the Radical 'pantheon' such as Paine and Henry Hunt. In 1838 he was one of the prime movers behind the formation of the Newport Working Mens Association, and his work as a bookseller and newspaper agent helped to inform and educate the local population about political affairs generally and Chartism in particular for more than a decade, but his most dramatic contribution was the frenzied period of missionary work to promote the Charter in Newport and the Monmouthshire valleys that he undertook in the first few months of 1839. Though he was undoubtedly outstripped in charisma and box-office appeal by Henry Vincent, his co-campaigner for part of the time, Edwards was a popular figure in his own right amongst working people, and David Jones believed that he 'had a particular affinity with the poorly paid'.[237] His efforts contributed to the recruitment of thousands of people to the Chartist cause, and he secured 'near ten thousand signatures' for the National Petition in sixteen weeks, and 'formed eight good (Chartist) societies'.[238] He provided a link between Newport, then the largest town in South-east Wales, and the population of its industrial hinterland, and he also had connections with Bristol and other parts of Gloucestershire. The influx of large numbers of colliers 'decisively proletarianised' South Wales Chartism according to Wilks,[239] and these recruits, many of them Welsh speaking, with their traditions of secrecy and coercion derived from the Scotch Cattle, provided many of the planners and rank and file marchers of the Newport Rising. Although Edwards was in gaol in November 1839, his work can therefore be considered to be influential in making the Rising possible.

In a letter to the *Midland Counties Illuminator* written from Oakham Gaol in March 1841, Edwards set out to explain what the Chartists were attempting to achieve, and in so doing he produced a detailed statement of his political beliefs.[240] The Chartists sought 'to have their own rights and no less', and the Queen and the aristocracy should 'have their rights and no more'. All men 'of full age and of sound mind' should have the right to vote by ballot, as 'that which concerns all men should be assented to by all men', and labour as well as property should be represented in the House of Commons: here he quoted William Godwin who wrote 'There is no real property in the world but labour'.[241] If the Charter became law, the result would be the election of 'a good and cheap government which would improve the conditions of the working classes'. All laws passed should protect the poor, as 'the rich can look after themselves'. Taxation and representation should 'go hand in hand', and 'the road to preferment and honour should be thrown open to all industrious, virtuous and intelligent men'. Edwards went on to list a number of actions which would be taken by a post-Charter government: the abolition of Church rates, the removal of Bishops from the House of Lords and the abolition of ecclesiastical courts - always likely to be favoured targets for someone of Edwards's religious beliefs; the banning of the impressment of seamen and of flogging in the army; the repeal of the New Poor Law; and the promotion of free trade 'with all the world'. He concluded with a demand that there should be the same law for the rich as for the poor, and for all men to be rewarded according to their merits: 'but they must obtain the Charter first'. In the same letter Edwards described how the Charter could be gained by using all possible legal means including petitioning and exclusive trading with sympathetic shopkeepers, and he emphasised the importance of education, discussion, and temperate habits, which would demonstrate that working class men were to be trusted with the franchise. It is apparent from Edwards's surviving writing that he placed no reliance on the ability of prominent individuals to deliver the Charter. On several occasions he emphasised the importance of united action, which gave working people 'power over those who controlled them', and said that Thomas Attwood's capricious behaviour 'should teach the Chartists not to trust in any one man but in themselves as a body'.[242] It is notable that Edwards made no mention of Feargus O'Connor, the most prominent Chartist of the period, in any of his letters, articles, or reported speeches.

Following his release from prison in 1841, Edwards continued his public advocacy of the Charter throughout the 1840s, and helped to ensure the survival of the movement in Newport after the trauma of 1839. His belief in universal male suffrage as a natural right rather than based on a sentimental commitment to reclaiming a mythical lost Anglo Saxon constitution, and his republicanism, place him firmly in the tradition of Tom Paine, though he differed from Paine when it came to religion.[243] In one of his letters from Oakham, he derided the idea of 'the ancient rights of the people of England', and said that he did not believe that 'the people of this country were ever in possession of their rights'.[244] He was remarkably steadfast in his views over many years, a characteristic which he shared with John Frost, and his last letter to the *Midland Counties Illuminator*, written two days after his release from Oakham, was a diatribe against Attwood's inconsistency as evidenced by his abandonment of Chartism.[245] One exception to this, however, was Edwards's attitude to the use of force to obtain the Charter. For all but a brief period in 1839 he clearly espoused peaceful, legal and constitutional methods of proceeding, but his language became more violent and incendiary between the Devizes riot on April 1st and his arrest in May. This change was short-lived, and while in prison and after his release he returned to his previous position: indeed in December 1841 he publicly condemned the Rising which his actions had done so much to bring about. It is likely that Edwards was carried away by the adulation of the large crowds attending his meetings in the spring of 1839, and was angered and provoked by the vicious treatment received by Vincent, his close friend and colleague, at the hands of the mob in Devizes. His role in the 1841 general election was a stain on his record, and it seems likely that his financial problems made him vulnerable to bribery by Reginald Blewitt. But even those most bitterly critical of him at that time seemed to forgive and forget, perhaps a testimony of good will towards him previously built up among his colleagues. For his part, Edwards was obviously able to work constructively with long term political opponents, as evidenced by his membership of the committee of the Mechanics Institute where he served alongside a number of figures from the anti-Chartist Newport establishment: this was probably made easier by his absence from Newport at the time of the Rising.

Edwards's sister Mary and both of his wives were involved in the campaign for the Charter, and there is evidence from his writing and from reports of his speeches that he supported the involvement of women in politics, although there is no record that he ever called for full female suffrage. Mary was a member of the Newport Female Patriotic Association, a parallel body to the Newport Working Mens Association, and she and Sarah kept Edwards's book and newspaper business going during his imprisonment. Ann, Edwards's second wife, was a shareholder of the Chartist Land Company. Edwards's *Address* from Monmouth Gaol was directed to the *Working Men and Women of Newport and the Monmouthshire Hills*, and in the text he quoted Paine: 'These are the times to try men's souls', but added 'and women's too'.[246] As we have also seen, in a public meeting in 1843 Edwards proposed that women should be involved in the fight against the education clauses of the Factory Act.

As far as Edwards's character and life outside politics are concerned, he appears to have been a committed Nonconformist, spending one and possibly two periods as a licensed dissenting preacher, and his religious belief is also apparent in the frequent references to the Bible in his letters and speeches and in his style of oratory. Looking back from the viewpoint of today's increasingly secular society it is easy to overlook the centrality of faith in the lives of people like Edwards. There is no doubt that his religion, and especially the particular version of Nonconformity which he followed, had a major influence in determining his ideas about politics and justice. At one time he appears to have been a heavy drinker,[247] but he renounced alcohol while serving his prison sentence and, just as in his consistent adherence to his political beliefs, he appears to have remained a teetotaller until 1843 at least. He seems to have been psychologically robust despite the *Merlin's* taunts, and coped well with incarceration, the public humiliation of the 1841 election, and the death of his first wife. He had at least four children, who undoubtedly suffered financially due to his political activities, and his apparent difficulty in running his bookshop successfully, as evidenced by the stock sale to pay creditors in 1845, his subsequent attempt to combine the sale of fruit with his core business, and his eagerness not to lose all the money he had invested in *Sam Sly* when he appeared before the magistrates in 1849. There is no doubt that his decision to become an active Chartist and his steadfastness in that cause adversely affected his life in a number of ways: as he wrote in 1841, 'I have suffered in my mind, in my character, in my circumstances and in my person on account of my Radical principles'.[248]

Any biographical writing such as this involves an exercise in empathy and imagination: the author tries to see through the eyes of their subject, and to walk in their footsteps. The 1840s Newport townscape familiar to Edwards has almost vanished, with only a few isolated buildings such as St Pauls Church, the Murenger House and the castle surviving, but the street layout is more or less intact and despite much rebuilding, the house numbers of Commercial Street have not altered since they were first established in the mid nineteenth century.[249] We also have a number of drawings and photographs which enable us to visualise the town at that time. As can be seen from this study, we can discover much about Edwards himself from official records, newspaper reports, his trial appearances and the recollections of his friends and colleagues, but in one respect he remains a ghost or shadow in his own story: there is no known surviving image or portrait. A whole gallery could be filled with pictures of many of the men he encountered in his life - though none of the women - including political allies and opponents, judges and barristers, members of parliament, government ministers and even the Newport registrar who signed his death certificate, but of Edwards's physical appearance we know little. There are references to his large physique, but nothing more: his hair, his features, the clothes he wore are left to our imagination. Despite this deficiency, I hope that this account has gone some way, in E. P. Thompson's phrase, to reclaim Edwards 'from the enormous condescension of posterity',[250] and restore him to his true status as a serious, influential and durable presence in the story of South Wales Chartism, a man who did his best to improve the lives of others, often to the detriment of his own circumstances. Perhaps the last word should be left to William Edwards himself, who wrote as he was about to leave prison in 1841: 'I pledge myself to dedicate my time, my talents, my influence and the energies of my mind to the great work of destroying error in all its forms, and of defending and publishing the truth in all its beauties'. [251]

NOTES ON THE TEXT

INTRODUCTION

1 These are the first two lines of the third verse of the hymn 'In Gabriel's hand a mighty stone' by Isaac Watts, 1674-1748.

2 W. E. Adams, Memoirs of a Social Atom (1903), Chapter XX. Adams was referring to South Wales in general, but Newport was the eye of the storm.

3 Chris Williams, 'Foreword', p. xv, in David J. V. Jones, The Last Rising (Cardiff, 1999).

4 GB Historical GIS / University of Portsmouth, Bristol UA/City through time | Population Statistics | Total Population, A Vision of Britain through Time. www.visionofbritain.org.uk/unit/10056676/cube/TOT_POP Accessed 27th July 2021.

5 G. Farr, West Country Passenger Steamers (1967), pp. 62-64.

6 Western Vindicator (hereafter WV), 23rd February 1839.

7 'The Queen against Henry Vincent and others 1839', in Reports of State Trials, New Series (HMSO, 1891).

8 The term 'packet boat' was applied to vessels conducting regular freight or passenger trade, and derives from their original function of carrying mail.

9 WV, 4th May 1839.

EARLY LIFE

10 Edwards, WV, 20th April 1839.

11 WV, 20th April 1839, 27th April 1839.

12 According to the first national census, Itton had a population of 86 in 1801.

13 Gwent Archives, 'Itton Baptisms 1773-1812', reference LDS/PA 1; John Edwards, will: NLW reference LL/1833/39.

14 Gwent Archives, 'Shirenewton Burials 1798-1859', reference LDS/PA 36: 2 Jan 1833 EDWARDS John residence Itton age 67; 1 May 1839 EDWARDS Mary residence St Arvans age 76; Gwent Archives, 'Itton Baptisms 1773-1812', reference LDS/PA 1.

15 Monmouthshire Merlin (hereafter MM), 18th December 1841.

16 Ivor Waters, About Chepstow (Newport, 1952), pp. 61-68.

17 Shirenewton Monumental Inscriptions, transcribed by Dave Woolven, transcript images supplied by Gerry Pritchard.

18 WV, 20th April 1840, 27th April 1840.

19 Bristol Archives, 'Records of the Anglican Parish of St James: marriage register 1820-1825', reference P.St_J/R/3/11.

20 National Archives, 'Stroud, Old Meeting, Gloucester, Denomination: Independent: Births and Baptisms', reference RG 4/1074.

21 The Act of Toleration 1688 (1 William and Mary c 18) received Royal Assent in May 1689. british-history.ac.uk

22 John Edwards: will, 1833; NLW reference LL/1833/39.

23 Midland Counties Illuminator (hereafter MCI), 27th March 1841.

24 R. Lawton, 'Rural Depopulation in Nineteenth Century England', in Dennis Mills, ed., English Rural Communities (1973).

25 John Edwards: will, 1833; NLW reference LL/1833/39.

26 J. Williams, Digest of Welsh Historical Statistics (Cardiff, 1985), Volume 1, p. 322; Volume 2, p. 31.

27 Ibid, Volume 1, p. 64.

28 G. T. Clark, Report to the General Board of Health on a Preliminary Inquiry into the Sewerage, Drainage, and Supply of Water, and the Sanitary Condition of the Inhabitants of the Borough of Newport (1850), pp. 16-30.

29 J. M. Scott, The Ancient and Modern History of Newport (Newport, 1847), pp. 71, 93; J. Matthews, Historic Newport (Newport, 1910), pp. 242, 243.

30 D. Thompson, Chartism and the Chartists: Popular Politics in the Industrial Revolution (1984), pp. 106-108.

CHARTIST ADVOCATE: 1838 - MAY 1839

31 Edwards, Northern Star (hereafter NS), 9th February 1839.

32 bl.uk The People's Charter.

33 www.chartistancestors.com ; the Six Points were: universal male suffrage over the age of 21, equal electoral districts, a secret ballot, no property qualification for MPs, payment of MPs, and annual parliaments.

34 E. Royle, Chartism (1993), pp. 21, 24.

35 WV, 20th April 1839.

36 Ibid.

37 Ivor Wilks, South Wales and the Rising of 1839 (1983), pp. 113-114; MM, 3rd August 1839; Evidence of Morris Morris, shoemaker and former member of NWMA in 'The Queen against Henry Vincent and Others 1839' in Reports of State Trials, New Series (HMSO, 1891).

38 MM, 27th October, 3rd November, 17th November, 1st December 1838; WV, 20th April 1839.

39 M. Chase, Chartism: A New History (2007), p. 45.

40 Jones, The Last Rising, p. 57.

41 Ibid, p. 59.

42 MM, November 23rd, 1839.

43 NS, 9th February 1839.

44 NS, 23rd February 1839.

45 WV, 30th March, 6th April, 27th April, 4th May 1839.

46 WV, 16th March 1839.

47 NS, 28th November 1840; the petition was due to be presented to the House of Commons on May 6th by Thomas Attwood, but some last minute reservations on his part caused a delay until June 14th.

48 Chase, Chartism: A New History, pp. 97-98; M. Roberts, lecture, 'The Material and Visual Culture of Chartism', delivered at Newport Chartist Convention, November 2018.

49 WV, 20th April 1839.

50 WV, 27th April, 4th May 1839; MM, 20th April, 27th April 1839; Glamorgan, Monmouth and Brecon Gazette and Merthyr Guardian (hereafter GMBGMG) 27th April 1839.

51 MM, 4th May 1839.

52 WV, 6th April 1839.

53 WV, 4th May 1839.

54 MM, 20th April, 4th May 1839; WV, 27th April 1839.

55 NS, 23rd February 1839.

56 'Bastiles' was a term used for workhouses constructed after the passing of the New Poor Law in 1834.

57 Evidence of Watkin Richards, Thomas Hawkins, Thomas Phillpotts and Thomas Phillips in 'The Queen against Henry Vincent and Others 1839', in Reports of State Trials, New Series (HMSO, 1891), pp. 1053-1059.

58 NS, 9th February, 23rd February 1839; MM, 9th March 1839.

59 NS, 23rd February 1839.

60 WV 16th March, 6th April, 4th May 1840.

61 WV, 4th May 1839.

62 Jones, The Last Rising, p. 61.

63 WV, 4th May 1839.

64 WV, 6th April, 13th April 1839.

65 The Silurian, 18th May 1839.

66 WV, 20th April 1839.

67 MM, 13th April 1839.

68 WV, 27th April 1839; MM, 4th May 1839.

69 NS, 4th April 1840.

70 GMBGMG, 27th April 1839.

71 MM, 4th May 1839.

72 MM, 18th May 1839.

73 J. and T. Gurney, The Trial of John Frost for High Treason (1840), pp. 517-518.

74 WV, 27th April 1839.

75 MM, 27th April 1839.

76 Wikipedia entry for Sir William Courtenay.

77 National Archives, TS 11/502, letter from Sienkin ap Howell ap Edwards ap Jones of Nantyglo to the editor of the Glamorgan, Monmouth and Brecon Gazette and Merthyr Guardian, April 1839.

78 MM, 4th May 1839.

79 MM, 4th May 1839.

80 Programme, The Forbidden Hymn: A People's Opera (1989).

81 MCI, 27th March 1841; NS, 18th March 1839, (reprint of report from The Times).

82 MCI, 27th March 1841.

83 NS, 18th May 1839, (reprint of report from The Times).

84 NS, 18th May 1839; The Silurian, 18th May 1839.

85 WV, 25th May 1839.

86 Jones, The Last Rising, p. 80; NS, 18th May 1839, (reprint of report from The Times).

87 The Cambrian, 18th May 1839; H. J. Davis, A Short Account of the Rise and Progress of Newport (1891), p. 10.

TRIAL AND PRISON: MAY 1839 - MARCH 1841

88 Edwards, NS, 28th November 1840.

89 www.bankofengland.co.uk

90 WV, 18th May, 8th June, 15th June, 22nd June, 29th June, 6th July, 13th July, 27th July, 10th August, 24th August, 7th September 1839.

91 The People's History Museum in Manchester holds an archive of 51 letters written by Henry Vincent (VIN 1/1/1 to VIN 1/1/51) including 13 written from Monmouth Gaol and others written while he was in Oakham Gaol.

92 VIN 1/1/16, June 1st 1839.

93 National Archives, HO 18, letter from Charles Ford dated 2nd July 1840.

94 A copy of the pamphlet is held in the collection of Newport Reference Library, reference number M160 (342).

95 Matthew 12.30, 'He that is not with me is against me'.

96 Acts 1.19, Judas 'acquired a field with the reward of his unjust deed, and falling headfirst he burst open in the middle and all his intestines gushed out. This became known to all who lived in Jerusalem, so that in their own language they called that field Hakeldama, that is, "Field of Blood"'.

97 The Charter, 30th June 1839.

98 J. Cannon, The Chartists in Bristol (1964), p. 8.

99 NS, 28th November 1840.

100 This section, unless otherwise referenced, is taken from 'The Queen against Henry Vincent and Others', in Reports of State Trials, New Series (HMSO, 1891).

101 The Hereford Journal, 7th August 1839.

102 Wikipedia entries for Thomas Talfourd (1795-1854) and John Arthur Roebuck (1802-1879).

103 The Hereford Journal, 7th August 1839.

104 The Silurian, 18th May 1839.

105 The Hereford Journal, 7th August 1839.

106 MM, 3rd August 1839.

107 MCI, 27th March 1841.

108 Quarterly Medical Officers Report for Monmouth Gaol, April 4th 1840; Gwent Archives QSP & R 0017.

109 Magistrates Observations 20th October 1828 - 13th November 1841; Gwent Archives Q/MG/2: entry by Charles Marriott, August 3rd 1839.

110 National Archives, HO18, letter from Vincent, Edwards and Dickenson to Lord John Russell, dated August 20th 1839.

111 National Archives, HO18, letter from Charles Marriott to Lord John Russell dated August 11th 1839.

112 Hansard HL Deb 22nd August 1839, Volume 50, pp. 483-484.

113 Hansard HC Deb 2nd June 1840, Volume 54, pp. 895-908; VIN 1/1/21, 15th February 1840.

114 WV, 21st September 1839.

115 Peoples Collection Wales; Petition of Henry Vincent and others, Monmouth Gaol, 1839.

116 MM, 17th August 1839.

117 The correspondence referred to in this paragraph was published in WV, 28th September 1839.

118 National Archives, HO18, letter from John Frost to Home Secretary.

119 Magistrates Observations 20th October 1828 - 13th November 1841; Gwent Archives Q/MG/2; entry by John Vaughan, November 9th 1839.

120 VIN 1/1/21, 15th February 1840.

121 David Williams, John Frost: A Study in Chartism (1939), p. 256.

122 VIN 1/1/21, 15th February 1840.

123 All this section, except where referenced, is from NS, 4th April 1840, and MM, 4th April 1840.

124 Wikipedia entires for John Gurney (1768-1845) and Codrington Edmund Carrington (1769-1849).

125 VIN 1/1/23i, 28th February 1840.

126 Hansard HC Deb 2nd June 1840, Volume 54, pp. 895-908.

127 Ibid.

128 GMBGMG, 18th April 1840.

129 www.knowledgeoflondon.com

130 www.choleraandthethames.co.uk

131 Hansard HC Deb 2nd June 1840, Volume 54, pp. 895-908.

132 VIN 1/1/29, 17th June 1840.

133 MCI, 27th March 1841.

134 Hansard HC Deb 2nd June 1840, Volume 54, pp. 895-908.

135 National Archives, HO18, letter dated 5th June 1840.

136 National Archives, HO18, letter from James Wade, surgeon at Millbank Penitentiary, dated 2nd July 1840.

137 NS, 4th July 1840; MCI, 27th March 1841.

138 National Archives, HO18, letter from Oakham, no signature.

139 National Archives, HO18, letter from Vincent to Normanby dated 17th June 1840; VIN 1/1/29, 17th June 1840.

140 NS, 4th July 1840.

141 VIN 1/1/35, 22nd September 1840.

142 MCI, 20th February 1841.

143 National Archives, HO18, letter from William Orridge to Fox Maule dated 3rd July 1840.

144 The Mirror of Parliament, 1840, Volume 5, pp. 4467-4498.

145 NS, 28th November 1840.

146 www.chartistancestors.com

147 MCI, 20th February; 13th March; 20th March; 27th March; 3rd April 1841.

148 Ibid.; NS,18th July 1840.

149 C. Godfrey, 'The Chartist Prisoners, 1839-41', International Review of Social History, Vol. 24, No. 2 (1979), pp. 189-236.

150 National Archives, HO 40, Monmouth, pp. 599, 605, 606: two letters from Thomas Jones Phillips to Lord Normanby.

151 John Edwards: will 1833; NLW reference LL/1833/39.

152 Ibid; NS18th July 1840.

153 Godfrey, 'The Chartist Prisoners, 1839-41'.

154 NS, 26th December 1840, 30th January 1841.

155 Godfrey, 'The Chartist Prisoners, 1839-41'; NS, 28th November 1840.

156 NS, 28th November 1840.

157 MCI, 20th February 1841.

158 MCI, 27th March 1841.

159 N. Newitt, The Who's Who of Radical Leicester, on nednewitt.com

160 Godfrey, 'The Chartist Prisoners, 1839-41'.

161 Thomas Peronet Thompson (1783-1869) was Governor of Sierra Leone from 1808-1810. He was an opponent of slavery, and was sacked when he threatened to expose the scandal of freed slaves being forced into compulsory fourteen year apprenticeships. Thompson later became an MP, and supported universal suffrage.

162 National Archives, HO18, letter.

163 Ibid, letters dated 1841.

164 MCI, 3rd April 1841.

FREEDOM

165 Edwards, MCI, 20th February 1841.

166 Leicestershire Mercury, 27th March 1841; NS, 27th March 1841.

167 D. G. Wright, Popular Radicalism: The Working Class Experience 1780-1880 (1988), p. 126.

168 D. Osmond, 'After the Rising: Chartism in Newport, Monmouthshire, 1840-48' (University of Wales MA Thesis, 1994), p. 89.

169 Wikipedia entry.

170 MM, 12th June 1841; NS, 12th June 1841.

171 MM, 12th June 1841.

172 NS, 1st August 1840.

173 Williams, Digest of Welsh Historical Statistics, Volume 2, p. 129.

174 Pigot's Directory of Monmouthshire 1835; The Silurian, 3rd July 1841.

175 MM, 3rd July 1841; Monmouthshire Beacon, 3rd July 1841.

176 MM, 3rd July, 10th July 1841; NS, 10th July 1841.

177 National Archives, HO18, letter from Charles Marriott to Lord John Russell, dated 11th August 1839.

178 MM, 10th July 1841.

179 MM, 17th July 1841.

180 NS, 24th July 1841.

181 R. Wallace, Organise, Organise, Organise: A Study of Reform Agitations in Wales, 1840-1886 (Cardiff, 1991), p. 44.

182 MM, 10th July 1841.

183 MM, 10th July 1841; Monmouthshire Beacon, 3rd July 1841.

184 MM, 17th July 1841.

185 NS, 24th July 1841.

186 Monmouthshire Beacon, 21st August 1841.

187 MM, 10th July, 14th August 1841.

188 National Archives, HO18, letter from Reginald Blewitt to Normanby.

189 MM, 3rd July 1841.

190 MM, 17th July 1841.

191 NS, 21st August 1841.

192 MM, 17th April 1841.

193 NS, 27th November 1841.

194 The Welshman, 10th December 1841.

195 GMBGMG, 11th December 1841.

196 Osmond, 'After the Rising', p. 97.

197 MM, 18th December 1841.

198 NS, 5th February 1842.

199 NS, 26th March 1842.

200 In January 1842 during the First Anglo-Afghan War, more than 16,000 people - British and East India Company troops and civilians - attempted to retreat from Kabul to Jalalabad. Only a handful survived. (Wikipedia entry, 1842 Retreat from Kabul.)

201 MM, 7th May 1842.

202 MM, 1st April 1848.

203 General Register Office, death certificate of Sarah Edwards. (EDWARDS Sarah Dec 1842 Newport Vol. 26 Page 70 [age 46]).

204 www.titiudorancea.com ; ncbi/nlm.nih.gov

205 MM, 19th November 1842.

206 General Register Office, marriage register entry for William Edwards and Ann Eliza Williams. (EDWARDS William Sep 1843 Chepstow Vol. 26 Page 43).

207 As a comparison, Waterstones bookshop in Newport has around 30.000 books on its shelves (personal communication from Louise Hartwell, Manager).

208 P. Pickering, 'Chartism and the "Trade of Agitation" in Early Victorian Britain', in S. Roberts, ed., The People's Charter: Democratic Agitation in Early Victorian Britain (2003), p. 26.

209 M. Roberts, Chartism, Commemoration and the Cult of the Radical Hero (2021), pp. 6, 65.

210 MM, 13th July 1844.

211 Osmond, 'After the Rising', p. 66.

212 MM, 15th February 1845; Scott, The Ancient and Modern History of

Newport, Monmouthshire.

213 GMBGMG, 6th November 1841; Osmond, 'After the Rising', p. 98.

214 MM, 7th May 1842; Pigot's Directory of Monmouthshire 1835; Kelly's Newport Directory and Tide Table for 1848.

215 MM, 6th May 1843.

216 MM, 7th May, 10th December 1842.

217 Manuscript Committee Minutes of Newport Mechanics Institute 1843-1870, Newport Reference Library.

218 Newport Mechanics Institute Regulations (1842), Newport Reference Library.

219 MM, 1st April 1843.

220 MM, 5th August 1843.

221 GBMGMG, 22nd April 1843.

222 GMBGMG, 27th May 1843.

223 Chris Williams, '"Decorous and Creditable": The Irish in Newport', in Paul O'Leary, ed., Irish Migrants in Modern Wales (2004), pp. 58-60.

224 R. Kirkpatrick, 'The Mystery of William Caffyn', Bear Island Books blog.

225 Cardiff and Merthyr Guardian, 19th May 1849; MM, 19th May 1849.

226 Chartist Trial Depositions, vol. 24, pp. 64-65: unsigned draft letter to Lord Normanby, accessible at Unlocking the Chartist Trials on peoplescollection. wales .

227 General Register Office, death certificate of William Edwards. (EDWARDS William Sep 1849 Vol. 26 Page 106 [age 54])

228 historylearningsite.co.uk

229 MM, 21st July 1849.

230 Leicestershire Mercury, 21st July 1849.

231 Kelly's Newport Directory and Tide Table for 1838, p. 17.

232 Personal communication from Frances Younson, Gwent Archives.

233 Tabernacle Congregational Chapel, Commercial Street, Newport; Births Marriages and Deaths (CD): Gwent Family History Society (2011).

234 Passenger Lists of Vessels Arriving at New York, 1820-1897.

MAD BAKER OR MAN OF PRINCIPLE?

235 MM, 7th May 1842.

236 Wilks, South Wales and the Rising of 1839, p. 138.

237 Jones, The Last Rising, p. 81.

238 NS, 28th November 1840; MCI, 20th February 1841.

239 Wilks, South Wales and the Rising of 1839, p. 99.

240 Unless otherwise stated, this paragraph is derived from MCI, 20th March 1841.

241 William Godwin (1756-1836) was a political writer and radical. The quotation is taken from An Enquiry Concerning Political Justice (1793), which was written as a response to the French Revolution. Godwin married Mary Wollstonecraft: their daughter Mary married Percy Bysshe Shelley and was the author of Frankenstein.

242 MCI, 20th February 1841; 3rd April 1841.

243 Roberts, Chartism, Commemoration and the Cult of the Radical Hero, p. 114.

244 MCI, 13th March 1841.

245 MCI, 3rd April 1841.

246 The same quotation from Paine, without the reference to women, was used by Franklin D. Roosevelt when he addressed the American people after the bombing of Pearl Harbour. C. Hitchens, Thomas Paine's Rights of Man (2006), p.142.

247 Jones, The Last Rising, p. 74.

248 MCI, 27th March 1841.

249 House numbering began in the 18th century in Britain, and initially the clockwise or horseshoe system was used, as in Commercial Street. The numbers increase sequentially along one side and then back up the other, so that the highest number stands opposite number 1.

250 E. P. Thompson, The Making of the English Working Class (Penguin, 1980), p. 12.

251 MCI, 27th March 1841.

PICTURE CREDITS

Cover The image shows Westgate Square, Newport in 1860, engraved by Edward Buckler. This is the view, with the Westgate Inn on the left, which would have greeted anyone leaving William Edwards's shop at 173 Commercial Street. The cover background is based on the Chartist flag designed by Hugh Williams of Carmarthen, which was inspired by colours used by the Gorsedd of Bards: green symbolising the earth, white representing peace and justice; and blue symbolising heaven.

4 Bristol Steam Packet Wharf, Newport, in the 1840s. Published in J. M. Scott, *The Ancient and Modern History of Newport, Monmouthshire* (Newport 1847). Image supplied by newportpast.com.

16 Samuel Etheridge. Watercolour, artist unknown. Reproduced with permission of Newport Museum and Art Gallery.

20 Henry Vincent. Mezzotint by George Dawe, 1842 or after. Published by permission of the National Portrait Gallery, London. NPG D39356.

28 Town Dock, Newport, 1842. Lithograph by James Flewitt Mullock. Reproduced with permission of Newport Museum and Art Gallery.

31 Kings Head Hotel, High Street, Newport, 1837. Illustration published in Newport Encyclopaedia in 1937, artist unknown. Image supplied by newportpast.com.

37 Monmouth County Gaol prior to 1865. Image accessed from Wikimedia Commons.

39 Shire Hall, Agincourt Square, Monmouth. Lithograph, 1860. Image accessed from Wikimedia Commons.

52 Thomas Duncombe, MP. Pencil and watercolour, by James Warren Childe, 1836. Published by permission of the National Portrait Gallery, London. NPG 1651a.

71 Commercial Street, Newport, 1860-1863. Artist unknown. Image published in R. Nichols, *Monmouthshire Medley Volume Three* (1978).

73 Town Hall, Newport, 1843. Engraving, artist unknown. Published in the Illustrated London News, February 11th, 1843. Image supplied by newportpast.com.

ACKNOWLEDGEMENTS

I owe a debt of gratitude to the many people who have helped to untangle the buried threads of William Edwards's life. Ray Stroud and Sarah Richards have been bloodhounds on the trail of the Edwards family tree, and several times picked up the true scent when my searches were wandering in the wrong direction. Ray and Les James have always been ready to discuss the themes brought to light by the unfolding story, and have been great sources of constructive advice. Pete Strong alerted me to the existence of Henry Vincent's Monmouth gaol letters, and Sylvia Mason has been as puzzled as I have by the difficulty of discovering more information about Mary Brewer. Colin Gibson of Gwent Archives has been a willing fount of information about the newspapers and periodicals of the Chartist years. Joanne Cox of the British Library went well beyond the call of duty to find and copy for me Edwards's letters to the Midland Counties Illuminator, and Frances Younson of Gwent Archives did her best to track down his burial place, albeit ultimately unsuccessfully. Thanks to Rob Smith for his work on the map, Andy Dark for the cover, and to Olly Blackmore of Newport Museum and Nigel Young of Newport Past for supplying good quality copies of some of the illustrations. This book has been a family effort: my son Tomos patiently devised the layout in his valuable spare time, while my wife Julia contended with hours of laptop research and keyboard tapping on my part while working on her own projects at the other end of the table, and our two cats only occasionally rebelled against the neglect they felt they were enduring. Every effort has been made to ensure that the final text is as accurate as possible, but any residual errors and all interpretations of the evidence are mine alone.

INDEX

SIX POINTS PUBLISHING

Our name is derived from a popular chant regularly heard at meetings held indoors and outdoors during the early years of Victoria's reign. Launched on May 8th 1838 in London, the People's Charter gained the support of millions for its six constitutional reforms – a package intended to win the right to vote and turn MPs into delegates of the people.

Our Aim

To produce and promote high quality books that explore nineteenth century Radicalism, the ideas of Chartism and their historical antecedents, the movement's context and development into modern times. We seek to provide a voice for the diverse and cutting edge research that the Annual Chartist Convention at Newport has inspired and showcased since 2007 and the 'Chartist Stories' that CHARTISM eMAG has trailed since 2013. We wish to collaborate with interested individuals, historical societies and heritage bodies throughout Wales and beyond. Alongside new writing, we plan to publish out-of-print texts. In the immediate future, we are seeking joint projects with Newport Museum and Art Gallery, Monmouth Shire Hall, Gwent Archives and Our Chartist Heritage.

Coming in 2022

Les James & Sue Allen: *Son and Daughter of Argoed: Zephaniah and Joan Williams - Coal, Beer and Chartism.*

Six Points' Future Plans

Future plans include books about Henry Vincent, and also about the less well known South Wales Chartists, such as Jenkin Morgan, Wright Beatty and William Davies; a reprint of *The Rise and Fall of Chartism in Monmouthshire* by E. Dowling (1840); a critique of W. N. Johns: *The Chartist Riots at Newport, November 1839*, (1889); Chartist School Pack; and a publication on the commemoration of the Chartist Rising.

Six Points Publishing is brought to you by:

Les James
Ray Stroud
David Osmond
David Mayer
Sarah Richards
Dr. Joan Allen